## About the Author

Nick has been a professional editor and amateur writer for most of his adult life, and a 'cricket tragic' since boyhood. He has now found the time to fulfil a lifelong dream of writing a cricket book. Nick lives in the English-like village of Bathurst in South Africa's Eastern Cape Province. He considers himself a 'global citizen' in most respects and especially as concerns cricket.

# Bites of Cricket

# Nick Cowley

# Bites of Cricket

Olympia Publishers
*London*

**www.olympiapublishers.com**
OLYMPIA PAPERBACK EDITION

Copyright © Nick Cowley 2024

The right of Nick Cowley to be identified as author of
this work has been asserted in accordance with sections 77 and 78 of
the Copyright, Designs and Patents Act 1988.

**All Rights Reserved**

No reproduction, copy or transmission of this publication
may be made without written permission.
No paragraph of this publication may be reproduced,
copied or transmitted save with the written permission of the publisher,
or in accordance with the provisions
of the Copyright Act 1956 (as amended).

Any person who commits any unauthorised act in relation to
this publication may be liable to criminal
prosecution and civil claims for damage.

A CIP catalogue record for this title is
available from the British Library.

ISBN: 978-1-80439-729-9

This is a work of nonfiction. No names have been changed, no
characters invented, no events fabricated.

First Published in 2024

Olympia Publishers
Tallis House
2 Tallis Street
London
EC4Y 0AB

Printed in Great Britain

# Dedication

I dedicate this book to my wife, Cherryl, who has displayed infinite patience, encouragement and support during the writing of this book; to my late father, Bob, who was responsible for most of my earliest memories of cricket; and to my nephew, Patrick, who shared many of the more recent cricket memories (and constantly recurs in these Bites).

# Before Play

Have you known anyone to be "stumped and bowled" or "delayed hit wicket" – or at least be dismissed in ways that could be so described? Have you heard a musical box on a cricket field? Have you ever seen a batsman on crutches? What's the funniest thing you've seen on a cricket field? Have you watched what you considered to be the Worst Ball Ever, or reflected on who was the Unluckiest Player Ever? Did Shakespeare allude to cricket? Cricket is so full of the off-beat, the bizarre, the humorous, the unpredictable, the debatable, and much more, that I decided to try to capture instances of all these things – whether witnessed personally, read about or heard about – in a half-century of 'pieces', plus two (the number of Bradman's Test innings, if you like).

A major problem was what to call these 'pieces.' I toyed with many possible words. Reflections? Thoughts? Musings? Impressions? Sketches? Essays? Vignettes? Each of these words sounded too stilted or old-fashioned. I've settled on Bites, not just for the echo of the very twenty first-century word 'byte', but also for the food analogy. Cricket could be seen as like an enormous, delectable, mouth-watering dish, a vast edifice of a cake perhaps; and each Bite is like just one mouthful of that dish.

A few points informed these Bites. Please read them before you start eating, or rather reading.

**1. Humour** is found more in cricket than in any other sport. Humour is also very important to me. You'll find plenty of it here, ranging from wordplays and wry or hilarious anecdotes to irony, tongue-in-cheek comments, dry observations, allusions reaching outside cricket, and more. My tone is mainly light-hearted, though I treat serious topics with the necessary gravity.

**2. Timewarp** is the best word I can find for my sense (shared with many cricket lovers) that the game has a sweeping continuity alongside all the vast changes of the past sixty years; that its present often blends almost seamlessly with its past; that its history is more relevant than is the case with any other sport. Many of my Bites trace incidents and themes that recurred decades or a century apart. I don't give more dates than necessary and avoid all nostalgia. In the interests of topicality, I generally start with the most recent incident, match or player, and work backwards in time. At times, though, I depart from this reversed chronology.

**3. My sources** are an eclectic mix drawn from a lifetime of watching cricket, whether live at every level or on TV (okay, TV is also live in a sense, but you know what I mean) and reading, hearing and talking about it, more recently online. Nothing is invented, except for one jaunt clearly marked as 'CriFi.' Points of fact generally come from the authoritative site Espn.cricinfo.com, which I call Cricinfo for short. Many items, especially anecdotes, come from guest speakers at the now sadly defunct South African Cricket Society, or from my own memories of watching cricket. Others come from the countless cricket books I have read; I acknowledge these and the authors as far as I can remember them. Some of these books are long out of print. You are not going to encounter tired cricket tales that every fan knows. Where a story is old, I've generally reworked and placed it in the fresh context of an original theme. And a good many of these tales are almost forgotten by now and well worth reviving.

This is not an academic work, so I have no footnotes or references, other than bracketed cross-references between different Bites.

**4. My perspective** is international and objective. Much of my material deals with South Africa, as I know its cricket (and tortuous history) best as a lifelong resident; but everything is given a global resonance and context. England and English cricket feature in many Bites, and there is also plenty about every other major cricketing country.

**5**. A few points of **abbreviations and style.** SA is self-evident. ICC obviously refers to the International Cricket Council, rather than Criminal Court. MCC is the grandly named Marylebone Cricket Club based at Lord's, which used to play the seminal roles of governing English cricket and sending out England touring teams under its name, and still drafts and amends the Laws of the worldwide game.

'Saffer' is the nickname widely used around the sporting world for South Africans, though it is seldom heard in the country itself. I use it regularly in these Bites for convenience and as another way to enhance the global perspective.

Male pronouns are used as a rule for convenience, with apologies and absolutely no disrespect to the highly significant women's game (which has its own section and Bite).

The term 'batter' is preferred to 'batsman' from now on, partly because it's gender-neutral (a key policy change made by Cricinfo in 2022); but also because it belongs to cricket's past, present and, very probably, future. Accounts of eighteenth-century cricket talked of 'batters' long before either the word 'batsman' or the sport of baseball came into existence (I have a little fun in one Bite with the use of 'batter' in either cricket or baseball, as you'll see). Today, 'batter' is increasingly used in cricket; but it has long been the preferred word of many blunt-talking players and even commentators. And in the future, I expect the term 'batsman' to fall entirely into disuse.

6. This **very personal work** stems from personal interaction with cricket for most of my life. All judgments, opinions, interpretations and views are my own, unless otherwise stated. At the same time, I believe that you'll agree with, or at least note with interest, most of my assertions.

Enjoy.

Nick Cowley

(nick.cowley.npc@gmail.com)

# A. THE BIZARRE, HUMOROUS AND OFF-BEAT

# 1. 'STUMPED AND BOWLED'
## (Not in any Law)

There is, of course, no such way of getting out, and never has been. Law 39 is quite clear that only the wicket-keeper may perform a stumping. But I did watch one dismissal that was actually described this way (not as a serious scorecard entry) by a reputable reporter. It came amid the highest company. I was watching live at Lord's during the fabulous MCC vs Rest of the World match (see **Bite 46**). It happened like this.

Graham Gooch came well down the pitch to the West Indian off-spinner Roger Harper and drove very hard back to the bowler. The ball came back just as fast, almost as if it had hit a squash wall, so quickly did Harper stop it and shy at the stumps. Such a throw is very often just an act of aggressive 'showboating' by a bowler, but not this time: Harper saw a real chance of a run-out and achieved it perfectly. Gooch, a big man, couldn't turn round fast enough and was floundering like a (see next paragraph) as Harper's pinpoint lightning throw bounced on the pitch, deftly missing all of Gooch's bulk, and hit the stumps.

So what was the best comparison for what Gooch looked like at that moment? Coming from Africa, I thought of a large antelope, perhaps an eland, bolting for cover as a lion threatened it. An English newspaper reporter, however, was far less kind to the great opener in his article. He compared Gooch to a "stranded whale." The same reporter (whose name I forget) remarked that the dismissal really deserved to be recorded as *stumped and bowled Harper* to reflect the bowler's brilliant role. This I agreed with. At least the scorecard habit of including the fielder responsible for a run-out had already begun, so this dismissal goes down in the record as "Gooch, run out (Harper)" – a pale shadow, but nevertheless some reflection, of what happened. Someone on an online cricket forum in 2022 called this the best fielding by a bowler ever. He posted the YouTube to back his claim.

I described it all later to my English host that hot summer of 1987, a fellow cricket lover. His wife, who had little interest in the game, was within earshot. She picked up on the names and commented that it all sounded like a high-fashion party, involving the Gucci brand along with Harper's magazine. We laughed at the clever wordplay. But what I really thought, was that this was somehow fitting for a high-end piece of cricket in a very high-end match.

# 2. 'DELAYED HIT WICKET'
## *(The hardest umpire's call of all?)*

Ben Stokes swung lustily to leg, with such vigour that his bat flew from his grip, up, up and away into the sky over Lahore, then began to drop like an aerial bomb threatening the square-leg umpire. As Stokes, batless, trotted a leg-bye – part of England's sixth and last extraordinarily rapid fourth-innings chase of 2022 (see **Bite 27**) – somebody watching with me, asked "If the bat had fallen on the wickets, would he have been out?" "A good question", was all I could reply.

Appeals for what I am here calling 'delayed hit wicket' are nightmares for umpires to rule on, more so than any call on LBW or caught, because of the hugely subjective interpretation and application of Law 35 required of them. It provides, in brief, that the batter is out if he breaks the wicket with an action he takes "in receiving a delivery", but is not out if he breaks the wicket after he "has completed any action in receiving the delivery". Pity the poor Third Umpire, to whom the on-field umpires will often pass the buck. Instead of being able to use DRS technology to judge impact and trajectory, he has to decide almost existential questions of when one action ceases and the next begins, questions that would tax the greatest expert in philosophy or biomechanics.

Fortunately for umpires, scenarios that call for such a ruling occur very rarely. There have no doubt been a number of cases, but I have been able to find only three, two at international level and one in an English county match, with an informant telling me about a fourth.

In 2021, Zimbabwe captain Brendan Taylor crouched slightly as he tried to upper-cut a short one during an ODI against Bangladesh in Harare. Straightening up from the attempt, he lowered his bat and managed to brush off a bail. The fielders appealed and the Third Umpire agreed with them, sending an annoyed-looking Taylor on his way. Bangladesh would probably have won the match and the series anyway.

Australia's classy Mark Waugh was trying to save the final Test at Adelaide in 1998 with only three tail-enders left for company, when a rampant Allan Donald hit him on the right forearm. Waugh, in obvious pain, stretched the arm to try to relieve the numbness, with his bat still held in that hand – and negligently extended the bat far enough to knock off the bails. South Africa were adamant: the forthright off-spinner Pat Symcox could be heard yelping "He's out!" like a schoolboy on a playground. The Third Umpire was asked to review and decide (some thought this a cop-out by the on-field umpires, as the facts were already clear enough). He ruled Waugh not out. A win in this Test would have given the visitors a share of the series. There were reports that a furious SA captain Hansie Cronje speared a stump through the door of the umpires' change-room, but I have never heard this confirmed (a photo of an invoice for the repair of the door sent to the SA camp would have been the media's jackpot as evidence). Waugh's twin brother Steve, who was leading Australia, shows a certain amount of uncharacteristic sympathy with SA in his account of the incident in his autobiography *Out of My Comfort Zone*.

Something very similar had in fact happened before, in English county cricket. "A Derbyshire batter named Revill, did not have the luck of the devil…" There was certainly potential for a limerick when Alan Revill was struck on the hand by the Surrey and England great Alec Bedser on a sportive Oval pitch. Much like Mark Waugh, Revill shook the hand to relieve the pain; unlike Waugh, he wasn't holding the bat with that hand. But he shook the glove right off; it fell on a bail and dislodged it. Surrey appealed and the umpires – without benefit of a backup official – conferred briefly and gave him out. I wonder if the umpires at Adelaide in 1998 knew about the 1953 Revill case (which I read about in a book of cricket oddities and confirmed by a Google search).

The ICC's lawmakers could try to amend Law 35, but they would never find a solution to this dilemma of when exactly a batter ceases to be liable to be out hit wicket. You could debate it endlessly.

(The Stokes bat-flying incident mentioned at the start prompted an online colleague to recall that Kumar Sangakkara was once out when his bat slipped from his grasp onto his stumps during an ODI against India. For me, this wasn't a case of '*delayed*' hit wicket', because it all happened instantly as Sangakkara tried to play an R.P. Singh delivery. It was more akin to the recorded instances of a batter being out when his cap or helmet fell on the wicket as he played the ball – the latter headgear famously claiming Kevin Pietersen against the West Indies' Dwayne Bravo in a Test, though Pietersen wouldn't have been out after a rule change in 2017 made the helmet or part of it exempt from hit wicket dismissals.)

Let's consider just the Waugh and Revill cases, which have the common factor that the batter reacted instinctively to a painful blow and broke the wicket with his equipment. Should Law 35 be made more explicit, and if so, how? It could be argued that bowlers should probably not be rewarded with a wicket for hurting batters, especially after the Phil Hughes tragedy. On the other hand, the risk of being hurt when a batter is facing a Donald or a Bedser is well known and accepted as part of the game. Leaving aside the moral issue, the limits of the batter's "action in receiving the ball" are again, something for philosophers or scientists to discuss, not cricket's legislators. So Law 35 is unlikely to be amended in any way that will resolve this kind of dilemma.

As definitive guidelines are virtually impossible for 'delayed hit wicket', umpires – with or without the benefit of TV replays – will continue to differ in their *ad hoc* verdicts on future incidents. A harder call for them to make is hard to imagine. Inconsistency in a type of ruling that is only required every few decades, as this one seems to be, is probably something cricket can live with.

## 3. BI-BOUNCER BALLS
*(Not just playground stuff)*

A ball delivered by Pakistan's Mohammed Hafeez during the 2021 T20 World Cup that bounced twice before being dispatched to the boundary by Australian David Warner, highlighted a fairly recent change to the rules. The amended Law 21.7, part of the revision of the Laws of Cricket in 2017, stipulates that a delivery is a no-ball if it bounces more than once before reaching the batter. Before that, a ball could bounce twice or more and still be legal. This wasn't playground stuff; even the best of adult cricketers can allow the ball to slip out of their hands. Two legal double-bouncers before 2017 linger in my memory for their outcomes. One of them could have changed the course of a Test series.

The Bangladesh captain in 2008, Mohammad Ashraful, was an all-rounder who could bowl either off-breaks or leg-spin; it's not clear which one he intended when he let go a ball that pitched halfway down and then a second time, barely above ground level, before reaching South Africa's AB de Villiers. AB, a scratch golfer, seemed to try to get under the second bounce with a sort of golfing sand wedge shot, intended to carry not to some nearby green, but over the boundary at Mirpur. Not surprisingly even for AB, he toe-ended it straight up into the air and Ashraful took a simple caught-and-bowled. AB lingered and looked at the umpires before walking; as he explained afterwards, he'd thought such a delivery was a no-ball and that he could hit it anywhere with impunity. In fact he'd anticipated the rule change of 2017 by several years; this incident may have contributed to it. SA conceded a 22-run lead in a low-scoring Test (de Villiers had been holding the first innings together, the only batter on either side to look comfortable on an uneven pitch). In the event, Jacques Kallis ran through the home side's second innings and SA's batters managed the conditions better the second time round to knock off a target of just over 200 for five wickets. But it could have been different. (The second and last Test of this series also contained something memorable: a 415-run opening stand between Graeme Smith and Neil McKenzie – to the delight of their common alma mater, Johannesburg's King Edward VII high school – which remains a world record for Tests at the time of writing.)

Another bi-bouncer, one I actually saw live, was far less significant and is only worth recounting because it provided an object lesson in how to punish such a delivery without risking dismissal; not that AB could have benefitted from it, as he would not be born for some years. Ian Tayfield of South Africa's former Natal province was an off-spinner like his famous uncle Hugh, though a chasm below him in ability and accomplishment (nothing to be ashamed of: Hugh Tayfield was regularly chosen as the spinner in an All-Time SA XI for decades, though Keshav Maharaj may have ousted him by now). I was watching at Kingsmead in Durban when the younger Tayfield let slip a very slow two-bouncer to the burly Transvaal all-rounder, Alan Kourie, who played both cricket and baseball for unofficial SA teams.

Kourie looked as if he could also manage field hockey as he advanced to meet the ball square on, picked a spot on the leg-side boundary between the fielders, and 'mowed' the ball along the turf to precisely that spot. The Kingsmead crowd's only reaction was a sarcastic "Great ball, Ian!" My point is that Kourie's was the perfect, returns-guaranteed way to handle this kind of ball before the 2017 rule change; AB was perhaps over-ambitious in thinking he could nine-iron a six from just off the ground, no-ball or not, even with his almost unique ability to conceive and execute outrageous shots.

There have been other cases. A farcical incident in Australia needs to be mentioned, if only because it's so much viewed on YouTube. *A triple*-bouncing delivery by the home captain, Mark Taylor – a non-bowler if ever there was one – trickled into the stumps behind Angus Fraser's attempted 'mow'. Strictly speaking, Fraser should have been out under the rule of the time, just as de Villiers was; but it was a light-hearted Prime Minister's XI match, and umpire Simon Taufel overruled Law 21 and gave Fraser not out, apparently on the grounds of 'the spirit of cricket'. Taufel would not have done this in a Test match; but then, neither would Taylor have bowled himself.

The 2017 rule change was a good one. Six-year-olds playing in parks will now put in enough effort to avoid bowling bi-bouncers as soon as a parent, coach or even older child tells them that such deliveries are illegal. At a higher level, what happened to de Villiers was a travesty of cricket's natural justice (or of the spirit of cricket if you like), and perhaps he felt vindicated when he heard about the change. I presume he did; one of the duties of coaches, managers and players themselves is to ensure that the players are familiar with even obscure points of the Laws. That was something AB learnt for himself at Mirpur.

# 4. WHEN STREAKING STOPPED PLAY
## *(Indecent exposure or innocent invasions?)*

Actually it wasn't the direct act of streaking, but a common rain interruption that had stopped play on the occasion I remember most vividly in this regard. The rain had stopped some time before and the crowd, seeing no reason why play couldn't resume, were growing restless. Eventually someone took it upon himself to liven things up by 'streaking' – a new term at the time – onto the field. Buck naked, he eluded the only two security men and ran onto the covers spread over the pitch, possibly intending to cross the entire field for good effect. But the covers were soaking wet on top, and the streaker slipped, lost his footing and fell flat on his *back*. Revealingly, so to speak, he was lying face up, with more than his face on public display.

Whether he was out cold or too embarrassed to move, I cannot say. At last an official ran onto the field with a pair of trousers – a towel must have been deemed inadequate covering – helped the pitch invader to get dressed, and escorted him from the field. The crowd at Durban's Kingsmead stadium gave him rapturous applause, not least the female fans. He probably got off fairly lightly in those days, the late 1970s; today he would have ended up in court and received a heavy fine, at the least. This might be the funniest thing I have ever seen on a cricket field.

Streaking at cricket is apparently still seen in England; I've seen it reported by Cricinfo as recently as 2021 at a Hundred match, which provides the right sort of milieu. In South Africa, it persisted into the 1980s at least; and it overlapped with the arrival of floodlit matches in the popular and innovative Benson and Hedges limited-overs series. These factors combined in a bizarre way while a B&H match was progressing well into a distinctly chilly early-season evening. It was too cold for anyone to strip down completely; but a spectator retained his long-sleeved top garment while removing everything below it, and ran onto the field that way. I suppose it counted as a streak. There were some unkind comments about shrivelled prunes and the like.

South Africa has never actually seen testicles at Tests (that I know of); as the time of streaking at big matches (part of a general fad of streaking in tolerant societies like the US) fell during SA's cricket isolation. But these naked field intrusions happened fairly often during Test matches in England and to a lesser extent Australia; one famous photo showed a man vaulting over the stumps clad only in his shoes and socks.

All these exponents of exposure were male. To my knowledge, it was only in liberated Britain and perhaps only Swinging London that women ever streaked at major cricket matches (Australia is the only other conceivable country where it might have happened). One of them did it at a Lord's Test of all places. MCC members who'd been shocked when West Indian fans famously sang calypsos within the hallowed precincts in 1950, must have suffered apoplexy.

The Sun tabloid published two photos of the lithe liberated lady. One of them was widely circulated by other papers, showing her running naked as Eve on the sacred Lord's turf; the reaction of all the men already there is interesting. The one umpire visible has his eyes averted (*The umpire can't bear to look*, was the Sun's caption). Most of the players look merely bemused; but Ian Botham is squatting at first slip, hands clasped, with a broad grin on his face that manages to show approval of the girl's antics while stopping short of lewdness. The Sun's other photo of her (as anyone who has ever read the tabloid will have guessed) was on its Page 3 the next day, now lying down but still without a stitch of covering.

Streaking will not be seen at top-level cricket again; security at the biggest matches has evolved to a level unrecognisable from the old laxity, with officials posted every few metres along the boundary's edges. Transgressors of any kind are now dealt with ruthlessly (in passing, I do miss the days when spectators could flock onto the field during the intervals and study the roped-off pitch, commenting on it like seasoned critics, or play their own mini-games if they'd brought a bat and ball). In any case, streaking has long since gone out of fashion in society generally; some recent clothing fashions even away from the beach make it virtually redundant.

Players have also been known to strip down to the essentials, but generally well out of the public eye. TV coverage of cricket does not seem to feel the need to show voyeuristic views of a triumphant team in its change-room the way its rugby counterpart does, especially when the team has just won the Rugby World Cup. However, two cases of all-but-nudity involving leading South African players did play out more or less in public, and can safely be recalled now that they have no more than amusement value.

The SA win at Trent Bridge in 1965 remains memorable. It secured the first series victory over England since 1935 and was perhaps the greatest fraternal all-round achievement in Test history (as opposed to batting achievements by brothers): Graeme Pollock scored a rapid century and a fifty in a low-scoring match and Peter took a ten-for. What happened after the spectators had left, is less well recorded. Several of the SA players came out onto the field in nothing but their underpants (the white Y-fronted affairs of the time), drinks in hand, and pranced around the pitch in the twilight. Photos were taken; the negatives in those pre-digital days must have circulated widely, as the black-and-white pictures were still being shown off, naughty-schoolboy-style, in South African pubs and clubs for decades afterwards. I first saw them in the mid-80s in Johannesburg's venerable Old Edwardians club (where Graeme Pollock was still playing; you still heard disrespectful jokes about Pollock's Bollocks, as he was one of the players in the photos, unlike the more sober-minded Peter). By then, I was at an age when I no longer minded sights like that of my boyhood heroes clad in less than their customary immaculate whites; the photos would have seemed like sacrilege to me earlier.

The other instance was meant entirely for general public consumption right from the start, for it was an advertisement. Not every player would have posed for it, but Clive Rice had a rebellious and non-conformist streak in his youth that never quite faded as he reached the summits of South African and English domestic cricket. In his early 20s Rice enhanced his early reputation as an *enfant terrible* of the game with an ad that showed him lying on the ground wearing nothing but a strategically placed cricket bat. Interestingly, I can find no trace of this ad anywhere on the internet (I have forgotten the product it advertised). The obituaries of Rice that appeared after his untimely death in 2015 made no mention of the ad; it may be that the journalists who wrote them were too young to remember it, or felt that any mention would be out of place.

Public nakedness among players today would be punished with a severity far exceeding what stadium authorities would mete out on a spectator who tried to revive streaking. The fad is practically gone from the game. Whether it offended cricket's valued sense of decorum, or added to the rich humour of the game, you decide. But there can be no doubting the brazen bare cheek(s) of the perpetrators.

# 5. AN ITEM OF INTIMATE EQUIPMENT
## *("He's been struck amidships!")*

Everyone understands the protective function of a box all too well. Few occasions in cricket cause spectators to wince in sympathy with a batter more than when they see him struck right on the box and usually squatting on his haunches for a few moments until the acute pain eases. A Test batter, well into this millennium, suffered such a blow during a long innings and was asked about it by the commentators at the next interval. He replied in a very matter-of-fact way and with no hint of coyness, "Yeah, the boy down there really didn't like it." No cricketer in the modern era feels the need nowadays to talk in a roundabout or evasive way about the box and what it is for.

This wasn't always the case. Cricket boxes, and the earlier reticence about mentioning them, have given rise to some very funny stories and memories. First though, an expression regularly used by certain former commentators known for their eloquence. Drawing a metaphor from naval warfare (perhaps from a time when Nelson was an admiral and not a term for the 111-score dreaded by superstitious cricketers), these commentators would exclaim of a stricken batter, "And he sinks down on his haunches – the poor chap's been hit amidships!"

The forthright Australian great Keith Miller no doubt called a box a box. On one occasion, he reportedly – and credibly – had no qualms about removing his box on the field after being 'struck amidships'. What followed was later described by the commentator and writer Peter West as one of the most hilarious things he ever saw on a cricket field. West, however, couldn't bring himself to write the word 'box.' Instead, he used a circumlocution that I've borrowed for the title of this Bite: "Miller used his bat handle to do on-field running repairs on an item of intimate equipment."

A well-groomed young cricketer of days past was acutely embarrassed when he walked into a sports shop to find an attractive girl working at the counter. He stammered in a roundabout manner "Ah, uh, actually, no, well, yes, I'd like to buy a... a... you know, one of those, ah, a protective device!" The girl's brow cleared and she shouted to a colleague in the recesses of the shop, "Gentleman wants a box, can you bring 'em out, Alf?"

One last story on this tender topic, which I find hard to believe but did read somewhere, now forgotten. A player at club or at the most county level – it must have been in England – found himself wearing a box that gave a metallic clang whenever it was hit. After the first time, the bowlers naturally did their best to 'ping' him – quite literally in this case – just there, while the spectators roared with laughter at the repeated audio effect. It must have sounded like someone playing a one-key xylophone. The incensed 'butt' of the jokes (not quite the right word here) later stormed into the sports shop where he'd bought the offending item, threw it down on the counter, and yelled at the staff (who may have included a woman as in the earlier tale), "Look here, I asked you lot for a cricket box, not a flippin' musical box!"

Since the days of cod-pieces in the Middle Ages, this

particular wardrobe item in its changing forms has been the subject of much broad and often bawdy humour. And here as always, cricket does humour better than other sports and indeed most fields of human activity.

# 6. GREEKS PLAYING CRICKET
## (*Could cricket have a Nick Kyrgios?*)

We sat around a table on the edge of a large gravel square in the middle of Corfu town, sipping ouzo and watching a cricket match in progress practically under our noses. The boundary was unmarked, merely a notional line that appeared to pass beneath our table and others. It suddenly became much less notional when a swarthy fielder chased a good hit: he dived under the legs of a table, upset it and all the spectators' drinks, and retrieved the ball, all with much swearing in Greek. Despite his utmost efforts, the umpire signalled four runs; and the fielder's reaction to this was worthy of Ancient Greek drama. He gripped the shoulder on which he'd dived in apparent agony, clearly meaning to indicate to teammates and spectators alike how he'd given his all in his efforts to save the boundary. The performance could have come from a Greek warrior wounded in the fighting around Troy.

This episode (yes, it really happened; I still have the match programme in Greek and English) sprang from the long history of cricket on Corfu, a product of British control of the island for a century. It is or was recently still played there, mostly by expatriates, but also by some locals like that excitable fielder. Uniquely, much of the Corfiote cricket vocabulary is not English but Italian, and very descriptive Italian at that: a yorker, for example, is a *primosalto,* 'first-bounce'. This must stem from the prevalence of Italian while Corfu was under Venetian rule right up to the arrival of the British after the Napoleonic Wars.

Corfu's games have a flavour of their own (sadly not described in Gerald Durrell's vivid account of life on the island, *My Family and Other Animals,* though the TV spin-off *The Durrells* did include a cricket match). However, Greeks have played much more serious cricket as a result of their people's diaspora to Britain and many Commonwealth countries. Two Greeks living in the Southern African region who played Test cricket are noteworthy, one for his achievement at the Parthenon of cricket and the other for a curious statistical record. In keeping with the adjective most often applied to Ulysses/Odysseus of Trojan Horse fame, *polymetis*, which translates roughly as 'man of many tricks', both were spinners.

Xenophon Balaskas, known (especially to England batters) as 'Bally Balaskas' in the slang of the time, played for South Africa at Lord's in 1935 and cleaned up England with his leg-breaks and googlies, with match figures of 9-103. The win gave the tourists a shock series victory (SA's first in England and the only one up to 1965) and started a long tradition of SA winning at Lord's.

Athanasios John Traicos – his Greek first name is never used – had four nations contributing to his identity. He was born in Zagazig, Egypt, as part of the once large Greek community in that country. His parents emigrated to the then Rhodesia (now Zimbabwe), which at the time played cricket as part of the South African provincial setup. Traicos, an off-spinner, studied at a South African university, where he was coached by Balaskas in a strange coincidence. Eligible to play for SA on two grounds, Traicos was selected for the powerful but spin-light home team that whitewashed Australia 4-0 in 1970.

Traicos did not make much contribution to that famous series win, except to snuff out one rare flicker of Australian resistance when he had the threatening Doug Walters caught at deep square-leg during an innings victory in Durban. (The only trouble was that the South African umpire, before the advent of neutral umpires, called "No..." without adding "...Ball!", explaining later that he had changed his mind in mid-call about the no-ball – small consolation to Walters.) Traicos went on to become a lawyer in Harare, captained the Zimbabwe ODI side in the 80s, and was still good enough to be picked for Zimbabwe at the age of forty-two when the country was admitted to Test cricket in 1992. This not only put him on the brief list of those who have played Tests for two countries, but gave John Traicos a world record unlikely to be surpassed – the longest interruption, a symmetrical twenty-two years and two hundred and twenty-two days, in an individual's Test career.

A third South African international of Greek extraction actually also played for Greece itself (an ICC affiliate) in Division Two of the European championship in 2012, well after his retirement from higher cricket. Nic Pothas, a talented wicket-keeper-batter, played no Tests, but once had to make a long dash from the Caribbean, where he was playing for South Africa A, to replace Mark Boucher in the senior ODI team for a series Down Under. (Boucher had somehow injured his hand while trying to cut biltong, a South African dried-meat snack that he could not have obtained very easily in quarantine-prone Australia).

It is strange, perhaps, that only Southern Africa seems to have produced international players of Greek descent. Sydney is said to be the city with the second largest Greek community in the world after Athens, and you would expect a few Australian

Greeks to have achieved the same kind of success in cricket as Nick Kyrgios has at tennis (perhaps without his notoriety). So far, there has only been one such state-level player I am aware of, Theo Doropoulos of South and Western Australia (and Wellington across the Tasman).

Greeks have in general assimilated extremely well to the cultures of the countries they have moved to, while also keeping up their ancestral traditions. It seems very likely that more Test players of Hellenic heritage will emerge (not necessarily in South Africa or other predictable countries: Joshua da Silva, a Portuguese-Trinidadian, is playing for the West Indies.) Along with the more sober qualities needed for Test cricket, such players may well exhibit that Greek exuberance of the Corfiote fielder I watched diving under the table, upsetting the drinks and theatrically hurting his shoulder in his effort to save a four.

# 7. BOUCHER'S THOUSAND-WICKET MYSTERY
## *(Did he really reach four figures?)*

The headlines were poignant enough when a freak injury behind the stumps in England ended Mark Boucher's playing career abruptly after fifteen prolific years as South Africa's wicket-keeper. Then it was discovered that he'd apparently caught or stumped 999 batters in international matches across the three formats. So near and yet so far; not quite on the same sport-shaking scale as Bradman ending his Test career four runs short of the 7000 Test runs he needed for a 100 average, but still a comparable razor-thin near-miss of a highly significant numerical milestone. Boucher addresses the matter himself in his biography. He explains how somebody recalled that he had actually taken one international wicket as a *bowler,* thus bringing his tally up to a round one-thousand.

Both South Africa and the West Indies had long since given up any chance of winning that high-scoring 2005 Antigua Test, with one first innings of almost 600 and the other almost 750, by the time Boucher shed his pads, came on as the 11$^{th}$ bowler for SA, and had Dwayne Bravo, the eighth century-maker in the match, caught at mid-on. Flippant attitudes from teams make no difference to statistical records: SA became only the fourth Test team to use a 'full house' of bowlers; and this is still one of only two Tests (by 2023) in which there have been as many as eight individual centuries. So Boucher, however tendentiously, had his four figures: he says in his biography that he was granted a golf club membership on the strength of it.

But then Cricinfo threw a curve ball (to mix sporting metaphors). The respected website's stats section showed, beyond room for error, that Boucher as an international wicket-keeper had had 998 victims, not 999. So he still fell short of the magic thousand, even if you counted the bowling wicket! Was there some sort of conspiracy to keep him stranded in three figures? Yet Boucher's biography and other sources continued to insist that the official figure was 999. I set out to try to resolve the conundrum.

No, I didn't pore through every relevant scorecard. I am no statistician, much as I respect those in this key profession for cricket, and wouldn't ask one of them to undertake such a trivial task. The solution came through a process of trawling through Twitter, Facebook and other unlikely social media sources for every reference to Boucher and his record. It turns out that, in the West Indies again in 2010, Boucher handed over the gloves and pads during an ODI to AB de Villiers, who was possibly being groomed even then for a successful future role behind the stumps. *Boucher then took a catch fielding at extra cover.*

So there you have it. Mark Boucher dismissed 998 batters (including repeats) in international games as a wicket-keeper, one as a bowler, and one as an out-fielder. It still adds up to 1000, though cricket statisticians apply strict criteria and you'll never find the magic four figures next to his name in any archive. If you want to make this into a Pub Quiz question, be careful how you word it. And I hope the former Proteas coach is still a member of that golf club.

Roman numerals are deeply embedded in cricket, at least

some of them – XI and occasionally XII and XV, even XXII's in the past. Boucher's initial M can be read as a Roman numeral, which, as it happens, denotes 1000. (His full initials, M.V., signify 1005, but let's not go there.)

# 8. GEORGE LOHMANN'S MISSING BAT
## ("The wily bowler Lohmann/Neither fast nor slow man")

A cricket poet's rhyming effort to describe George Lohmann's constant changes of pace is a great help in understanding the phenomenal success of, by one yardstick, the greatest bowler of all time. Less poetic reporters who watched the England and Surrey star often wrote about all the 'work on the ball' that Lohmann managed to get. This was a late nineteenth-century term for what we today call 'movement': in Lohmann's case, it seems to have included a seamer's swing and cut as well as a spinner's breaks, and all of them in both directions.

He *must* have been a quite exceptional bowler to record such absurd and unparalleled averages, even in a time of uncovered pitches and uneven opposition: under 11 for Test cricket (5.45 for his 35 wickets in three Tests against a fledgling South Africa) and under nine for his entire first-class career. Less formal stats show that he sometimes took 14-plus wickets in an *innings* against local XXII's while on tour with more-or-less England teams; this at least shows how far Lohmann towered above even other outstanding bowlers of his time.

Many batters were no doubt spared by the tuberculosis that afflicted Lohmann in his prime and forced him away from

London to South Africa and the dry air of the Karoo semi-desert. Driving across this vast scrub-covered plain, any real cricket fan really has to turn off the N1 highway, some 230 kilometres from Cape Town, and visit the small graveyard near the hamlet of Matjiesfontein. Lohmann's cricket-themed headstone, paid for by the distant Surrey County Cricket Club after the TB claimed him at only 36, is worth the stop, apart from other graves of significant historical figures. In my case, I used to continue this Lohmann pilgrimage at Matjiesfontein itself, because his bat was carefully preserved in a glass case in the foyer of the Lord Milner hotel there.

One year I was aghast to find the bat gone. I was told that the glass case had been broken and the bat stolen. In the lobby of a smart hotel in the middle of nowhere? Pull the other one. My suspicion is that it was sold to an eccentric cricket lover, possibly English, much like those billionaire art collectors who buy up masterpieces just to gloat over in their private galleries.

Lohmann, a professionals' professional (read Keith Booth's biography, on which I have drawn), had his differences with the cricket authorities of the time. I don't know if this had anything to do with the ICC, over a century later, taking seven years to induct Lohmann into its Cricket Hall of Fame, founded in 2009. He should surely have been in it from the first.

Another overdue tribute to Lohmann would be for whoever took his bat to return it for public display at some suitable venue. Matjiesfontein is perhaps a little remote, though appropriate to the last part of Lohmann's life. The Oval would be very appropriate; Lord's, Newlands, or indeed any major stadium would certainly do. If the perpetrator lives overseas, I should think South Africa will magnanimously give up its claim to this relic of, statistically at least, the greatest bowler.

## 9. APPEALS AND STYLE
## (*How's that for variety?*)

So much has been written about the different ways the standard appeal by a bowler is varied and vocalised – all part of the unendingly rich lore of cricket – that I didn't think anything new could be added on the topic. That was until I reflected on all the idiosyncratic types of appeal I'd experienced living in one cricket country alone. Some of them may be unique, or at least new to you.

*How's that, sir?* I actually heard this umpire-respecting form of appeal at one of those private ('independent') schools in South Africa that still derive much of their ethos from the British public school – straw-basher hats, houses, prefects, pupils politely greeting every adult they pass (when last did you experience that?). Adding 'sir' to an appeal seemed a little excessive, though, and I don't think it lasted very long. This happened before there were as many women teachers umpiring at school matches as there are now – I'd love to hear "How's that, ma'am?" from a big burly schoolboy bowler.

*How's that, how's that, how's that?* The triple repetition, sounding like some sort of ritual incantation, was actually heard in a Test match while I was watching on TV. The reason for Keshav Maharaj's strident insistence was probably that he needed to convince his teammates, even the eagle-eyed keeper de Kock, that there was anything in it. The West Indian tail-ender's forward lunge had apparently parried Maharaj's arm ball successfully and everyone was moving on to the next delivery. But the SA left-arm spinner was convinced that it had been marginally pad first. His captain went along with him, and DRS confirmed Maharaj's impression, saving the batter only because the ball was clipping the bails and was thus umpire's call on height. I have never heard a triple appeal like that before or since.

*How WAS that?* The emphasis that a leading Johannesburg club bowler put on the middle word of his appeals was unusual; his use of the past tense was probably more common. "HowAzat" seems to have been, and possibly still is, a common variation of "Howzat" in English county cricket at least (I base this on the cricket serials in British boys' comics that once reached South Africa, which seemed to reflect colloquial UK usage quite well.) The great cricket writer Sir Neville Cardus mentions one of those bowlers with the Northern English accent and grammar that he so loved recording, who used to appeal with "How *were* that?"

*Howzat* itself, sometimes as its cockney variant *Owzat*, is practically an accepted English word, enshrined in the names of cricket dice games, computer games, shops and much else. Above all, two noted Australian artists have used the word in their work. The pop group Sherbet had a 1976 hit song called Howzat. It seemed to be more about relationships than cricket (the key line goes "I caught you out, Howzat"); but it obviously needed a society with a cricket culture to resonate, and indeed reached No 1 in the charts only in Australia and New Zealand. Earlier, Jack Fingleton, a prolific Test opener and even better cricket writer, wrote a memorable passage about what happened when Yorkshire's England pacer Bowes appealed against him for LBW during a match against the 1938 Australian tourists in Sheffield (an extremely big occasion in those days). Factories and offices around the Bramall Lane ground had stationed staff in windows where they could watch the action; these observers swung round and relayed the home team's "Howzat" to their colleagues, who passed it on, until everyone for miles around was aware of the Yorkshire appeal and waiting for it to succeed. The umpire, a Lancastrian, had the temerity to rule "Naht oot." The reprieved Fingleton, who had an imaginative gift for vivid descriptions, never quite explained how he knew all this was happening from his vantage point in the middle.

The contracted forms "How?" and "Zat?" are very common, of course; indeed any kind of yelp at the umpire with clear intent will do. Brendon 'Baz' McCullum, the game's best-known coach as I write, in his former keeper role for New Zealand never seemed to pronounce more than a sharp "Yeah!" when he appealed for a stumping or a catch standing up. Many other Australasian players' appeals more or less defy phonetic description.

To conclude, a long-forgotten story from another era that is too funny to pass over in this context. A quick bowler who happened to wear dentures (false teeth) managed to dislodge them with the force of a real 'effort ball', which crashed into the batter's pads. The bowler, unable to utter any clear words, waved his arms and mouthed incomprehensible sounds, but his intent was perfectly obvious. The umpire, quick to see his opportunity, said to him repeatedly "I beg your pardon, I cannot make out what you're saying." The bowler eventually picked up his dentures from the pitch, replaced them and asked rather grittily "How's that?" "Not out ", replied the umpire – who no doubt dined out on the story for years until it entered the folklore of cricket.

# 10. BOWLING PECULIARITIES: ODD ACTIONS AND RUN-UPS
## (*From India's submariners to the bowler who carried library books*)

Indian all-rounder Kedar Jadhav, whose low-arm, bent-knee action ensures minimum elevation and 'sloggability' for his off-spinners, is sometimes jocularly called a 'submarine bowler' – but for me, he is not the only one in his country. India's and sometimes the world's No 1 bowler, Jaspit Bumrah, has a ramrod-upright action, but an unusual one. The main oddity, apart from the ambling walk that forms half of his run-up, is the way his bowling arm shoots straight up from the shoulder, ball in hand, just before delivery; I can almost hear a submarine skipper's command ringing out, "Up periscope!".

A few bowlers in every generation have distinctive actions and run-ups that stand out from the general orthodoxy. If you can walk into a stadium with play in progress and instantly recognise the bowler from his action alone, he belongs in this category.

The most peculiar action seen in South Africa probably belonged to a slow bowler. Paul Adams was a left-arm wrist spinner who took the term 'unorthodox' to a whole new dimension. He seemed to look at the ground as he bowled, and the effect was of arms flailing about like an insect caught in the spotlight. Indeed his nickname among his Proteas teammates around the turn of the millennium was 'Gogga', an Afrikaans Khoi-derived word for a slithering insect (the G's are the same throaty guttural sound as that in the surname of Australia's SA-born batter Marnus Labuschagne, if he were to pronounce it in his native Afrikaans). Journalists regularly described Adams' action as being like "a frog in a blender." Even more vivid was the description by an English reporter during the England tour when he made his Test debut, "Adams' action was like a man trying to change a tyre on a moving car after the brakes failed." (Sadly this was later given a local racist twist with the version "...like someone trying to *steal a hubcap* off a moving car" in an implied reference to criminal gangs operating on the Cape Flats, where Adams hails from. I heard the clean and humorous first version many years before the other one. With its British origin, it was clearly meant as an amusing and graphic description of his action with no offensive intent.)

Perhaps the most unorthodox, rather than peculiar, action seen in South Africa, however, belonged to one of its greatest fast bowlers and one of its two best ever all-rounders. Mike Procter (probably just behind Jacques Kallis as an all-rounder) bowled at express pace off what appeared in every way to be the wrong foot. Experts, including some who played with him, have explained that this was only an illusion created by his whirling arm speed as he delivered. I would not be so bold as to disagree with them; but the fact remains that something seemed to be out of sync as Procter bowled. Photos of his flying delivery stride, both feet off the ground, show quite clearly that the *right* leg is leading. Whatever the truth, I saw many of my peers, schoolboys in their early to mid-teens, stumbling and getting into tangles as they tried to emulate Procter's perceived action and bowl flat out off the wrong foot – mostly in the nets, as few tried it in a match situation.

Other bowlers in SA, less spectacularly unusual than those two, had memorable mannerisms in their run-ups rather than their actions. Fanie de Villiers, nicknamed *Vinnige Fanie* or 'Fast Fanie' from his pace and middle name Stefanus (the popular translation 'Fast Fanny' seldom made it to print), is best remembered today for "Fanie's Finest Hour", the 1994 Sydney Miracle. He had a distinctive run-up, his tall frame moving with both arms extended outward from the shoulders but then bent towards the ground at the elbows, forming two downward L-shapes with the ends of the L's, the hands, at hip height, with the right hand clutching the ball. The effect was of a student without a knapsack taking books back to the library, six or seven books tucked awkwardly under each arm. If you wanted to extend the fancy, the student was running to reach the library before it closed. Fanie was indeed 'bookish' in the sense that he was able to think many batters out in a way that might not have been guessed from his straightforward manner.

Spinners are less likely to have eccentric actions than quicker bowlers, the inimitable 'Gogga' Adams aside. An earlier exception was the Australian leg-spinner Clarrie Grimmett, who was said to perform 'hobgoblin' work in his run-up. This was reportedly best negated by the batter only looking up when Grimmett was about to deliver – a policy that presumably required timing as exact as the actual batting. More recently, India's Harbajhan Singh posted a video of a bowler who, exaggerating Harbajhan's own approach, waved both arms like a butterfly as he ran up – so upsetting the batter, less forewarned than those who had to face Grimmett, that he withdrew with as much indignation as if someone had walked across the sightscreen.

In contrast with all of these oddities, it's worth mentioning the most aesthetically pleasing run-up I have ever seen. A fast-medium bowler in SA provincial cricket named Sibley McAdam seemed to bounce springily along the turf as he ran in: a less exaggerated version of astronauts walking on the lunar surface in those special 'moon-boots'. The fearsome legendary English quick of the Body-line series and earlier, Harold Larwood, had a run-up that must have been something special, because so many critics of the time wrote about how notable it was. One cricket poet even soared to high-flown lines of praise: *"...Larwood's bounding run, and Woolley's rapier flashing in the sun"* (imagine anyone writing like that about cricket or any other sport today). 'Bounding run' could certainly have been applied just as well to McAdam, though it is doubtful whether, on the one hand, he could have put batters in hospital as Larwood did, or, on the other, inspired any spectator to poetry.

In more recent times, Dale Steyn has had perhaps the smoothest run-up and action, while Bumrah has the oddest. Too much uniformity is not good for cricket. Long may unusual bowling actions continue to add to the diverse, broad-church fabric of a game that is happy to accommodate the unorthodox.

# 11. THE WORST BALL EVER
## *("He's still walking back to Johannesburg")*

There have been countless terrible balls delivered in cricket, and judging the worst of them can only be a subjective and fairly light-hearted exercise. Context is crucial. One ball can give a match away: Australia's Shaun Tait once had only seven to defend in a Super Over that followed a high-scoring T20I against New Zealand (equal scores of 211), and started with a wide far down the leg-side that went to the boundary: five runs already banked and six balls still left. Or the delivery can be startlingly out of sync with the high expectations of the occasion. England's away defence of the Ashes in 2006/7 was eagerly anticipated after their shock win in 2005, but Steve Harmison began the series in Brisbane with a wide across the left-handed Langer to second slip. It seemed like a laugh-out-loud piece of farce in that context and set the tone for the rest of England's series.

The context for my – again very subjectively chosen – example was what would normally be seen as a formality: seven runs to defend off what was supposed to be the last ball of a limited-overs match. Transvaal (now the Johannesburg-based Lions) seemed to have secured an away win over their old provincial rivals Natal (now the Dolphins) at the latter's home ground of Kingsmead, Durban. The bowler had only to make sure that he sent down a legitimate delivery.

Transvaal's Richard Snell, one of the pin-up boys of SA cricket at the time with his gangling, dreamy look, had merely to bowl a legal ball to another pin-up boy, the legendary livewire batter-fielder Jonty Rhodes. Snell managed not to overstep, throw the ball, or bowl a wide – but his full toss/near-beamer to Rhodes was well above waist height. Rhodes pulled the no-ball for six, equalling the scores. Snell's surname actually means 'fast' or 'quick' in Afrikaans (indeed Richie Benaud on a visit as commentator, aware from touring as a player that South Africa had a Germanic language, pronounced Snell's name like the German word *schnell*, which has a similar meaning). But there was nothing fast about the way Snell, a normally lively seamer, trudged back to his mark, or about the desperate attempted slower-ball yorker with which he tried to retrieve his calamitous error (I forget the tie-breaking mechanism of the time, long before Super Overs). Though nowhere near as badly as with the preceding 'Worst Ball', Snell just missed his length. With the field up, Rhodes – more successful than Klusener in a similar and much more famous situation – turned it neatly to the midwicket boundary to clinch a Natal victory that had been inconceivable less than two minutes earlier.

During a post mortem of the game at work next day, a colleague commented in Afrikaans, "*Snell stap seker nog terug Jo'burg toe*", Snell must still be walking back to Johannesburg. His punishment probably wasn't quite as severe as that. But I would have loved to be a fly on the wall at Transvaal's next fines meeting. All the purveyors of the worst balls ever – and there must be an infinite number of other candidates – would have their own team reactions to compare with Richard Snell's. But they would probably all prefer to let those reactions stay, Vegas-like, in the dressing-room.

# 12. CRICKET'S MOST RESENTED WALK-OFF
## (*The political rebellion that spread to cricket*)

A walk-off in a cricket match is a serious matter. Some teams have left the field when the physical safety of the players appeared to be in danger, as has happened during riots in the Caribbean and in the sub-continent. Jack Fingleton's book *The Wildest Tests* records some of the most famous, or infamous, instances. In such cases the team that walks off is entirely exonerated by the mitigating circumstances.

Not so with another type of walk-off, involving a serious disagreement between a team and the match officials. Rishabh Pant incurred a fine (an inadequate sanction in the view of many) when, captaining a side in the 2022 IPL, he tried to 'call back' his players in protest against an umpires' decision. The Pakistan team left the field at The Oval in 2006 in protest against an umpire's accusation of ball-tampering, leading to the only match in Test cricket's long history deemed to have been forfeited by one side. The ICC flip-flopped on the matter, at one point declaring the match a draw, but later reverting to the umpires' original verdict that Pakistan had forfeited the Test.

Pakistan – as a team and nation – may have felt robbed, but that isn't the case I had in mind. A virtually forgotten walk-off in Southern Africa, and the administrators' subsequent ruling, had political ramifications. The whole episode is worth recalling for its bizarre nature and the issues it raised, if nothing else.

The country now called Zimbabwe, formerly Rhodesia and before that Southern Rhodesia, was happy to play as a South African province for most of the twentieth century, taking part in SA's domestic Currie Cup and supplying SA with a number of distinguished Test players. The national/provincial side was never quite strong enough to win the Currie Cup. Except in one season, and that led to an almighty blow-up, with the nation's political leader weighing in. First, however, a review of the purely cricketing details.

It all started with the question of when a day's play ends. Cricket used to do this purely by time stipulations: stumps would be drawn at 5, 6, 6.30, or whatever time the local daylight duration made suitable. Today, a hybrid of time factors and the number of overs to be bowled in a day is used. For some years in between, however, there was a 'Mandatory Hour' on the last day of a match if needed, under which 20 overs had to be bowled from the start of the last hour, however long they took, conditions permitting. The umpires, of course, had to indicate clearly when the last hour had started and the 20-over count had begun.

Which they apparently didn't in a Currie Cup match in 1972 between the then Rhodesia and Eastern Province (based in South Africa's Eastern Cape), played in the present Zimbabwe's western second city, Bulawayo. Briefly, the home side, batting last, reached what they thought was the 20$^{th}$ and last over with six needed to win and plenty of wickets in hand: a cakewalk, even in those days when run-a-ball was less commonplace than today. But Lorrie Wilmot, the visiting captain, believed that the 20 overs were up, and led his team from the field, claiming a draw.

Mike Procter, the brilliant South African all-rounder who

captained Rhodesia then and was batting at the end, having carefully managed much of the run chase himself, stormed up to the umpires and found them in complete agreement with him. The umpires (rightly, I believe) awarded the match to the home side, ruling that Eastern Province had forfeited it by declining to play on. But the South African Cricket Association, SACA, of the time, overruled that verdict few weeks later. This decision proved crucial for that season's Currie Cup, as the points for the win would have made Rhodesia champions for the only time in their history (instead Transvaal were crowned yet again). That was when politics intruded in a small but significant way.

This is not the place to recap the emotive, racially divisive, war-torn situation of Zimbabwe's forerunner state, which had unilaterally declared independence (UDI) but was regarded internationally as a rebel British colony. All that is relevant here is the reaction to the cricket fiasco of Rhodesia's leader at the time, Prime Minister Ian Smith. Trivial though a signal sporting success may seem in that troubled larger context, it would have helped the isolated state to assert itself and boost morale – but that had now been taken away by the Big Brother (though supportive) neighbour's cricket authorities. So another Rhodesian rebellion followed. *Prime Minister Smith had a replica of South Africa's cricket Currie Cup made, and awarded it to Mike Procter at a formal ceremony.*

Today, very few people remember the episode. Zimbabwe Cricket – a fully-fledged and independent ICC member for decades, though with some hiccups and interruptions – surely has no institutional memory of the matter. The officials, umpires and players involved are gone or probably wouldn't want to discuss it. It would be interesting to know whether Mike Procter kept that replica Currie Cup in his well-stocked trophy cupboard.

Walk-offs in cricket are highly undesirable and will continue to be extremely rare. If one does happen, a forfeiture ruling would be the logical and legal consequence. In that case it is likely that debate and strong feelings, even national passions, will accompany any future instance as they have before.

## 13. LOCAL RESIDENTS vs BRITISH TROOPS
## (*Did anything like the 'Lagaan' story ever happen?*)

This question has probably been asked ever since cricket's most popular film appeared in 2001. I'm not about to delve into all the vast research on the history of India under the British Raj or the rich history of cricket in the country, but will confine myself to the simple answer given in Quora and similar online platforms. *Lagaan* is fiction, but something like that could have happened under the prevailing conditions. From the perspective of the present day, when cricket is by far the favourite sport of the world's most populous nation, it's easy to imagine the villagers taking so quickly to the game they'd watched the British garrison play so often. And with remission of a hated and onerous tax, the lagaan, at stake, it wasn't too far-fetched to imagine they'd have been motivated to edge out the Army team in a desperate finish, despite having zero previous experience of a sport that the occupiers were steeped in.

Interestingly, the imagined scenario came closer to happening in South Africa, though admittedly there are many differences. The Afrikaners, earlier called Boers, had been 'local residents', with no home base in Europe, for two and a half centuries by the time British troops invaded their republics as part of the conflict known as the Anglo-Boer or South African War.

They'd had a good deal of contact with the adjacent British colonies and had taken enthusiastically to their sports, especially rugby (which remains a deep-set Afrikaner passion). Came the war, a senior Boer officer once sent a polite request to the defending British garrison commander at the Siege of Mafeking (still a famous episode; the town's name is now spelt differently). The Boer leader asked for a Sunday truce and social mingling between the two sides, specifically including a cricket match. The British commander (the Lord Baden-Powell who started the Scout Movement) liked the idea, but declined, saying the sterner match had to be completed first.

In the fictional *Lagaan* story, the unarmed and impoverished Indian villagers achieve a bloodless rout of the occupying forces, last seen in a retreating wagon convoy, by literally beating them at their (then) own game. The potential Anglo-Boer cricket match at Mafeking would probably have been a much more enjoyable and indeed cordial affair between combatants with little personal grudge against each other. In real life, sport has been able to alleviate warfare in this way on a handful of occasions, with the best known being the football games during the short-lived Christmas Truce between British and German troops in the first year of World War One.

Sport may be war fought by other means, but it's a damn sight preferable. And the advance from the fictional but historically-based fraught tension of *Lagaan* to the friendly rivalry of an India-England Test match today is a huge achievement, as is the hard-won unity of all South Africa's races in support of the Proteas and other national teams.

# B. DESCRIBING THE GAME

## 14. CRICKET WORDPLAYS
### (*Camilla Bowles, Mann's inhumanity, and others*)

Cricket, more than any other sport, has given rise not only to masterly writing but also to countless creative wordplays, whether in books, by spectators or elsewhere. Many of these are weak tabloid puns; but others are too memorable and clever not to pass on before they are forgotten.

Two of the game's best wordplays both deal with the same unpleasant theme – bowling with an illegal action, earlier known informally as 'throwing' or 'chucking.' The ICC rules on elbow flexion and technology-driven assessment and remedial procedures have done much to solve the problem. The unpleasantness it caused, did at least give rise to these clever puns.

Muttiah Muralidharan (correctly spelt with a D) is enshrined today as the only bowler to have taken 800 test wickets and highly respected for his great career and later his work with Shane Warne to promote spin bowling. But Australian crowds and umpire Darryl Hair (not a favourite of South Africans) were merciless towards Murali's action before the ICC finally cleared the double-jointed off-spinner as an entirely legal bowler for posterity. A riddling poster wielded by Australian spectators during the controversial 1995/96 Sri Lanka tour was perhaps the wittiest I have seen at cricket: *What's the difference between*

*Muralitharan and Prince Charles' love interest? At least Camilla Parker Bowles.* Even today, now that Charles is the British monarch, Camilla his queen consort, and Murali a highly respected elder statesman of the game – judged by some as greater than Warne - all three would probably enjoy wry smiles if they were reminded of that poster today.

An Ashes tour dogged by controversy gave rise to another vivid wordplay, this one a book title equally damning of certain home bowlers' actions. The Test opener turned journalist and author, Jack Fingleton, called his account of the 1958/9 series, won 4-0 by the home side, *Four Chukkas to Australia*. The polo term 'chukkas' was a bold pun on 'chuckers': for this series was marred by the questionable actions of a number of the Australian bowlers. (There was no other connection to polo, though a later MCC {England} team were accused of playing too much golf; their captain, 'Lord' Ted Dexter, excused his team's poor performance at a charity golf event with "I'm afraid we've been playing too much cricket").

Fingleton had a knack for clever wordplay in book titles. Apart from *Four Chukkas to Australia*, he called his book on Bradman's farewell tour of England in 1948 *Brightly Fades the Don* (an echo of the classic if voluminous Russian novel *Quietly Flows the Don*). And his book on the 1953 Ashes tour, when England reclaimed the trophy after 19 years, was titled *The Ashes Crown the Year* – probably intended as a triple wordplay, because the same year also saw Queen Elizabeth II's coronation and the conquest of Everest.

The Ashes, with the varied symbolism the concept carries in cricket and other contexts, have inevitably been worked into other cricket book titles employing wordplay, though Fingleton's is perhaps the best. The cerebral England captain Michael

Brearley, who took over from a struggling Ian Botham and then oversaw the great all-rounder's near single-handed defeat of Australia in 1981, called his book on the series *Phoenix from the Ashes*. This reflected not only Brearley's classical education but also Botham's red, like the mythical phoenix, from the figurative ashes of the first two Tests to the personal heights that won the cricket Ashes. And oddly it was not an Englishman or Australian, but a South African, the star batter Roy McLean, who titled a book *Sackcloth without Ashes*. This dealt with SA's worst defeat during McLean's thirteen-year Test career, a 4-0 home thrashing by Australia in 1957/8. His somewhat enigmatic title was possibly meant to suggest: (i) that South Africa's performance was mournful; and (ii) that there was no officially named trophy like the Ashes at stake for the third oldest Test rivalry. (There still isn't; Cricket Australia tried to find a name quite recently, possibly based on the Border-Gavaskar Trophy for its series with India. This exercise could easily have yielded the rather humdrum-sounding Smith-Smith Trophy, as Steve and Graeme came fairly close to overlapping as captains).

Much more light-hearted than these book titles are the slogans on posters that spectators draw up, sometime spontaneously, and wave for the TV cameras and all to see. Australian fans have a more-than-century-old tradition of witty and not-so-witty 'barracking' (you can read up on Yabba, the legendary rabbit hawker and merciless heckler whose bust still decorates what was once the Sydney Hill at the SCG). They also widely use rhyming slang like 'michelle' (Pfeiffer) for a fiver (bowling) and 'dorothy' (US journalist Dixer) for a sixer (batting). So Aussie fans easily converted this oral tradition to inventing some clever posters. We've noted the Murali/Camilla classic. Another nifty one referred to a vocal anti-immigrant politician, as well as to Michael Bevan, a batting stalwart who could also bowl left-arm wrist-spin, and to a now outlawed term for his stock ball: *Even Pauline Hansen likes Bevan's Chinaman (*see **Bite 36** on this term and type of delivery*)*.

South African cricket authorities and media, soon after returning to the international fold, tried to encourage similar wit by offering prizes for the best poster displayed in the crowd. The inspiration for one came when New Zealand left-arm spinner Matt Hart, who looked a little like the actor Colin Farrell, fluffed the simplest of catches at the Wanderers (though Hart later atoned by helping to bowl the Kiwis to a surprise victory in this 1995 Test). The winning poster appeared moments later, possibly drawn up by a group of female fans: it read, *MATT, you set our HARTs a-flutter; a pity you've got hands like butter*.

South African journalists came up with a very sharp wordplay based on the names of Peter May's MCC (England) touring squad of 1956/7. They pointed out that the visitors could have fielded a viable team whose last initials would have spelt *MCC WILL LOSE*: May, Compton, Cowdrey; Wardle, Insole, Laker, Lock; Loader, Oakman, Statham, Evans (with only five recognised batters and an attack of two pacers and three frontline spinners – one of whom had just taken 19 wickets in a Test – this team might conceivably have been picked in the sub-continent rather than SA).

The oral wordsmiths of the game, the commentators, have often come up with spoken wordplays. Perhaps the cleverest one ever came from the silver-tongued BBC commentator John Arlott (whom South Africa's wonderful Charles Fortune was said to resemble in style). When the South African left-arm spinner 'Tufty' Mann dismissed his namesake, the England captain George Mann, in 1949, Arlott came out with the gem

"*Mann's inhumanity to Mann*".

That was a conscious pun; not so the one commentator's gaffe that everybody in cricket knows. The man who unconsciously uttered "*The bowler's Holding, the batsman's Willey*", was just using a set formula for conveying information to radio listeners; he only realised what he'd done when the sniggering began in the media box around him. How wonderful it would be to recreate the famous gaffe with the offspring of the players concerned: but while Test batter and umpire Peter Willey's son David has often played for England, sadly Michael Holding's son Ryan has never followed his father's 'Whispering Death' footsteps into fast bowling, commentary or big cricket at all. Maybe a third generation will oblige...

Another commentator's unintended wordplay lay only in misinterpretation by the listeners that had startling consequences. A BBC radio channel was whizzing around the various county grounds for updates not too long after World War Two, when it crossed to Lord's, where J.J. Warr was captaining Middlesex. The update, "And the news here is that Warr's declared", was enough to cause many listeners to phone the BBC in panic and ask whom the war was against this time.

The same pun was inevitably made, though quite deliberately, decades later with the Waugh brothers at their peak. Steve and Mark had many fine partnerships together (during which the taciturn twins reportedly said little to each other in mid-pitch but a terse "Batted" after each milestone). The best of these, a 400+ stand for New South Wales in an away match against Western Australia, prompted a newspaper headline *Waugh breaks out in Perth*.

Memorable cricket wordplays seem to be less easy to find in recent years. A good rhyme (rather than pun) was sent to Cricinfo during an England middle-order partnership some years ago: "Stokes and Woakes are jolly good blokes." This rhyme would clearly invite an expansion if Ben Foakes and Chris Woakes ever play together in the Test team under Ben Stokes. No doubt some poetically gifted fan would oblige, possibly with a limerick.

Cricket offers abundant opportunity for wordplay, and it has the attention of many people from assorted nations with a sharp verbal wit and fine command of English. In this regard, be sure the game will not be stumped for very long.

# 15. GREYHOUNDS IN THE SLIPS
## (*and other Shakespearean cricket references*)

Apart from being respectively the best game and the best writer produced in England (you may delete the last three words if you like), cricket and Shakespeare have little obviously in common. We have to turn to our sketchy knowledge of cricket's early history to guess if it meant anything at all to Shakespeare: possibly he knew it vaguely as a mainly rural pursuit that involved using a shepherd's crook or 'creag' to defend a wicket gate from some sort of woollen or leather missile. Yet those who have read Shakespeare in the original for the past three centuries have most likely been people who at least understood cricket (outside North America).

So it's inevitable that every phrase in his work that could possibly be applied to cricket has been picked up. They amount to a mere handful, just four obvious ones in all, which have been noted by many writers. But those writers have added very little to the quotations, as far as I know; so I'm presuming to make a few observations, with the greatest respect to both the sublime source of these nuggets and all those who've scoured his plays and poems for them. I'm adding a fifth, for reasons that will become clear. The first two have to be considered together:

**A hit; a very palpable hit.** (*Hamlet*) **A touch, a touch, I do**

**confess.** (*Hamlet*)

These two quotes occur within a few lines of each other during Hamlet's supposedly friendly fencing bout with Laertes. The first is an umpire's call, in cricket terms. The word 'palpable' used to be a favourite of cricket reporters who disagreed with the umpire about whether a batter had got a snick, or nicked off as we say today. I often used to read something like "Milburn was lucky to survive a palpable edge when he was on 12". Given the prominence that Shakespeare used to enjoy in everyone's English syllabus, I have little doubt that these reporters were influenced by this very line in their choice of adjective. During a DRS process of the present day, some viewers would find it very satisfying if a Third Umpire reviewing the Ultra Edge line were to quote these Shakespeare phrases instead of the boring formulaic "Clear spike there; Kumar, I'm ready to give my decision". These viewers aren't holding their breath, though.

The confession of a touch would obviously come from a batter who chooses to walk, a species that DRS has made all but extinct and redundant (would any modern batter walk if he knew he'd touched it but the fielding side had failed to appeal, never mind review?) Pre-DRS, it's most unlikely that Adam Gilchrist or any other top-level 'walker' would ever have quoted the line when asked by a TV interviewer about his dismissal. But one can imagine a cricketing student, schoolboy, actor or anyone else exposed to *Hamlet* quoting the line even today, possibly in a semi-jocular tone – or if the umpire happened to be the schoolboy's English master.

**The most unkindest cut of all** (*Julius Caesar*)

This single phrase from Mark Antony's masterly oratorical hatchet job on Julius Caesar's assassins has trashed Marcus Brutus's image for ever. Brutus goes down in history as the ungrateful nephew who helped terminate his benevolent uncle with extreme prejudice, instead of the democratic tyrant-slayer he was trying to be. This is proof of Shakespeare's quite amazing influence on historical perceptions as well as our language. We barely even notice the double superlative 'most unkindest', as Shakespeare was as exempt from stuffy grammatical rules as a twenty first-century youth on a smartphone, but I'll stick to 'unkindest cut' for brevity. But can any connection be found with the cricket stroke whose name permits a vivid wordplay like "Bradman's footwork forced the bowlers to pitch short, and then he cut them to ribbons" (Neville Cardus, who didn't mind penning the odd pun if it was as apt as this one)?

My suggestion is the 'upper cut', that intrusion from boxing parlance that made fast bowlers' jobs much harder as white-ball formats forced batters to become more innovative from around 2000 onward. Before that, a slash over the slips was seen as a risky, lucky shot that encouraged the pacer to hope the next one would be hauled down by a leaping keeper or slip extending the cordon upwards. Since the evolution of the controlled, calculated 'upper cut', quick bowlers can only look on in frustration as perfectly good short balls are guided well above the slips and wide of third man for almost unpreventable boundaries. The shot is now seen regularly even in Tests and is even in the coaching manual (something that would have pleased the late SA opener Eddie Barlow, who regularly played the 'upper cut' and insisted it was quite safe and intentional, at a time when sceptics said he was lucky to keep getting away with it). So that could be cricket's 'unkindest cut', applying generally to the victimised fast bowlers of around 2000 and thereafter.

As a last word here, let's recall that cricket also had its Julius Caesar, who played for Surrey and the All-England XI in the

1850s. So that Julius Caesar was safe by some one hundred and fifty years from having to face a possible 'unkindest cut' at the hands of Marlon Brutus, who played for the waterfront and bounty-laden island of Sint Maarten in a T20 in 2006.

**I see you stand like greyhounds in the slips** (*Henry V*)

England's great warrior king Henry the Fifth, firing up his 'Band of Brothers' troops with the granddaddy and template of all pre-battle motivational speeches, is talking about a sport much older than cricket. Greyhounds were used for hunting and racing from at least Ancient Greek times, millennia before society 'went to the dogs' and started using them as a betting vehicle like horses. The slips King Henry refers to are the slip collars used to keep greyhounds in check until the moment you let them go. Shakespeare's image perfectly conjures up the coiled spring-like state of a human or animal poised to explode into action, like Henry's soldiers before tackling the French - or like anyone engaged in a reaction sport like cricket. The image could apply to a slip fielder, ready to throw himself at a ball that 'slipped' off the bat (the term used before anyone spoke of edges, snicks, nicks, touches or tickles). The hero of Shakespeare's *Henry V* – with his nickname Harry, rebellious attitude, red hair, wild youth, dangerous military service, foreign wife and conduct compromising his royal status (not permanently in his case) – has a very modern resonance within an ancient institution. So, whatever kind of slips the earlier royal Harry was talking about in Shakespeare's script, it's fitting to find in his words a link to our venerable but modern game.

**Single nature's double name, neither two nor one was called** (*The Phoenix and the Turtle*)

Huh? you ask. This line, like the entire Shakespeare poem from which it comes, describes two beings fused so inseparably that they are virtually one, but not quite. Any connection with cricket is owed entirely to the poet-author-academic Edmund Blunden. In his remarkable book *Cricket Country,* Blunden finds echoes of cricket in a range of literature and other arts. The echo he finds in Shakespeare here is so compelling that I've decided to include it, with full and free acknowledgement of my debt to Blunden. He is talking about the most famous opening partnership in the game – Hobbs and Sutcliffe, the 'Old Firm'.

Blunden, writing in the 1940s, had watched them extensively. To summarise, he sees them as a whole greater than the sum of its parts, a unit feared even more when together than as two separate batters both of legendary status. He tells us, as do others, that calls of "Yes" or "No" were barely heard between Hobbs and Sutcliffe: a glance at the partner was enough to tell if a run was on (did any of their Test partnerships, which averaged 87, ever end with a run-out?). Shakespeare's line was the best expression Blunden could find of this union based on absolute understanding.

I'll add a couple of original observations. Blunden here helps to rectify the almost instinctive subordination of Sutcliffe in cricket lore. We nearly always read and say "Hobbs and Sutcliffe", hardly ever the other way around, for a range of reasons. Blunden, using Shakespeare's mystical phrase to imply a union of absolute equality between the two batters, has at least done something to address this inequity. Much could also be written about the popularity of the mythical Phoenix in cricket: it appears in club or team names from Durban to Bengaluru to Birmingham, and also in one of cricket's better book titles, Mike Brearley's *Phoenix from the Ashes.* The poor Turtle, by contrast, is hardly seen in the game (unless you have time to play Doodle Cricket on your digital device). It's as unlikely to be a popular symbol in cricket as its fellow water-loving creature, the duck.

An adaptation to cricket of another famous Shakespearean quote is worth adding. At a time when England were still trying to replace Hobbs and Sutcliffe (!) and other top-order stalwarts, and the touring South African batter Dudley Nourse was reeling off centuries, an England selector wailed, "A Nourse, a Nourse, my kingdom for a Nourse" (see **Bite 37A** on Nourse).

Cricket gives enormous pleasure. Shakespeare gives enormous pleasure. Enjoying them both together is a treat, only occurring with these few faint echoes. Or we could add, "the play's the thing."

# 16. A BELOVED COMMENTATOR
## (*His Voice was his Fortune*)

"*The shadows are lengthening over the Wanderers in the late sunshine as Australia quietly play out the day. Goddard is really moving the ball – well, of course the ball is moving from Goddard to the batsman, but I mean to say he's making it move sideways, an appreciable distance both ways... And my goodness, a dog has run onto the field. Well, better the dogs come to cricket than cricket go to the dogs. A steward has removed the hound, a handsome Retriever, before it can try to retrieve the ball. I remember how a dog came onto the field at Lord's in 1965... Procter continues with what will be the last over of the day. In he runs, in he runs, and finally lets it go – Lawry shoulders arms like a guardsman on parade yet again as it curves away from him yet again, Lindsay gathers and makes some kind of signal. Procter walks back to his distant mark, a thoughtful look on his face... As I was saying, that dog at Lord's in 1965 managed to evade the stewards and had to be caught by a more fleet-footed player, I believe it was Bland... {Background crowd roar!} My goodness me, what has happened? He's bowled him! Yes, he's bowled him! Lawry's stumps have been knocked awry and he's trudging off, shaking his head, as Lindsay runs to bear-hug Procter...*"

You had to hear Charles Fortune's fruity, mellow tones for

yourself to capture the full flavour of his commentary. Many, not only South Africans, will remember his voice vividly; it was easily parodied. The above is a sort of collage meant to reflect his general style and capture some of his most memorable moments on the air. He would describe the scene with the most loving attention to detail, whether it was shadows dappling the ground or a dog running onto the field. He used exquisite language with a wide vocabulary, as might be expected of his other job, as English master at the venerable St Andrew's College in Grahamstown (now Makhanda), Eastern Cape. He understood the technicalities of the game perfectly, but preferred to express them with vivid figures of speech: a batter would never 'leave' or 'let it go' but always 'shoulder arms'. And yes, Charles did get so carried away with cricket memories or incidental descriptions that he occasionally missed a crucial piece of play and was brought back to earth, or the present, by an erupting crowd roar.

(SA paceman Mike Procter really did 'do' Australian opener Bill Lawry late in the day at the Wanderers in 1967 as described. The left-handed Lawry was letting Procter's 'bananas' swing harmlessly past his off-stump; so Procter, perhaps prompted by his keeper Lindsay, switched to round the wicket, changed his finger-grip, and immediately castled Lawry, who ignored the change of angle and fatally 'shouldered arms' again to one that held its own. Charles made up for his inattentiveness by quickly reconstructing what had happened for his listeners: everything but the change in finger-grip, which Procter himself revealed in a later account.)

Listeners forgave Charles an occasional lapse, even as big a one as that. There was no television in South Africa in those days, and his rare slip-ups were a small price to pay for his marvellous word pictures of the action. Few figures connected with South

African sport can ever have been held in the same kind of affection. He understood the game perfectly, and expressed it better than most. Hearing him exchange views on cricket with his peers from other countries – the Englishmen John Arlott and Brian 'Jonners' Johnston, the Australian Alan McGilvray – was an immeasurable treat. In an ideal world, the same would have applied with his West Indian, Indian and Pakistani counterparts.

Cricket commentary has virtually disappeared from South African radio stations today, a far cry from the ball-by-ball channel that used to be available. Apart from TV, online scores and commentary are the only resort. But if you are driving and want to catch up with the cricket, it's just too bad until the next sports bulletin on your car radio. As for TV, the commentators are mostly ex-players who very often give valuable insights (my favourites are Mark Nicholas and Nasser Hussain), but also often merely point out what is obvious on the screen. Charles Fortune was part of a bygone era. The game and the world have moved on. I've tried to avoid all hints of nostalgia and longing for 'the good old days' in these Bites, focusing instead on cricket's continuity amid all the changes. But I will make an exception in this case, especially as one would struggle to find a YouTube or audio recording of Charles today (the SABC sold most of its archives to a commercial broadcaster some years ago). Charles Fortune and his inimitable commentary are still missed.

# C. DISPENSING THE GAME'S JUSTICE

# 17. UMPIRES SURVIVE UPHEAVALS
## (*What role do they have in the 21$^{st}$ century?*)

Much umpire-player interaction is kept private, but Cyril Mitchley, a South African umpire who served on the ICC's Test panel, once let out the inside story of an instance that had commentators baffled at the time. Standing as Australia fielded in a tense Ashes Test in Sydney, Mitchley was seen to speak on his walkie-talkie (those two-way radio devices that umpires used to carry). He then called over the home captain, Ricky Ponting, and senior player Mark Waugh at the end of the next over. The commentators wondered whether the hard-bitten duo had done anything untoward. Perhaps Ponting and Waugh wondered the same as they approached the umpire. Mitchley seemed to ask them something, received a brief answer and then let them go. It was a mystery to all onlookers.

Mitchley explained the incident at a cricket function in South Africa some weeks later. The Melbourne Cup, Australia's biggest horse race, was on that afternoon, and in the spirit of doing as the Romans do, he'd jokingly handed an Australian official a 20-dollar note to stake on his behalf. Shortly before the off, the official had called him on the field via the walkie-talkie to ask which horse he wanted to back. Mitchley had no idea about the local equine form, but he knew exactly which players in the field could advise him – and summoned 'Punter' Ponting and the younger Waugh, both passionate followers of the 'nags'. The whole tale might seem improbable and too informal for Test cricket (it's hard to imagine it happening today); but I heard Mitchley relate the story himself as the guest speaker at a South African Cricket Society function. So I had it, well, from the horse's mouth.

Before drawing any moral, I will relate another story around the umpire-layer relationship, from a lower tier of the game. A provincial and occasional international cricketer was speaking at a SA Cricket Society function, at a time when top players could still take part in some club matches

"The umpire had stood in our club games for years and loved doing it. But he was getting old and had become so short-sighted he could hardly make a correct decision. He was becoming an embarrassment and it was time he went. But nobody wanted to hurt his feelings by asking him to retire. So we hatched a plan before a game." The speaker was careful not to name anybody or any team other than his own club side. We in his audience waited in suspense to hear about the plan and whether it had worked.

"We waited until the opponents had a tail-ender facing who never made runs and the bowling was from that umpire's end. Our bowler went through his whole action, but bowled – nothing. He just held onto the ball. The batsman stood there confused. But our bowler clicked his fingers as loudly as he could. (The speaker clicked his own fingers to illustrate). The keeper caught – nothing. But he threw up – nothing – and he and the slips all went up. So of course the half-blind umpire lifted his finger. The batsman wanted to say something, but then just went off furious."

"Of course there was hell to pay after the game. The other side weren't sure whether to complain to the League about us or about the umpire. We explained everything to them, in the umpire's hearing. Yes, it was brutal, but it worked. The next day was Monday and he went to the League and submitted his resignation." We all laughed our heads off, but you had to feel for the aged umpire. The story was too outrageous not to be true, and the speaker wasn't the type to fabricate anything like that. At least the end result was in the best interests of cricket.

Both stories in their different ways illustrated the contradictory position of umpires on the field. On the one hand, they are dreaded figures of authority and justice, 'robed' judges who can give a player out or cite him for a breach of discipline. On the other hand, they are human beings who like a little banter with the players, such as getting a racing tip from them, but they are fallible and can make serious mistakes. Cricket today offers more sanctions against an umpire who regularly gets it wrong than that nasty if hilarious plot against the myopic umpire. DRS corrects the bad decisions (though I do think the umpire must feel mortified every time he has to cross his arms over his chest, like a Scot showing the St Andrew's Cross or a supporter of South Africa's Pirates football club displaying his allegiance to the skull and crossbones.) But an umpire who is overruled by DRS too often will face the consequences. The team captains write reports on the umpires in which they will express any dissatisfaction – not limited to decisions on appeals.

Yet with all this, I feel that umpires are still the symbol of much that is valuable in cricket. As the sole judges of fair and unfair play, they safeguard the spirit of the game when anything happens to threaten it. They are treated with respect by players. Any player who transgresses is sanctioned, as happened to Josh Hazlewood when he once asked quite audibly after a referral went against his side, "Who the **** is the third umpire?"

Marginal decisions on DRS are still adjudicated according to the umpire's call, leaving them with a strong measure of authority. They in turn behave with dignity and respect for the game and its players. I always feel a glow of satisfaction when an umpire flicks off the bails at stumps and says not just "Over and Time", but adds "Thank you, gentlemen."

Arguments have been made for 'umpire's call' to be eliminated and all marginal decisions to trigger an automatic DRS process. Some cricket lovers would agree, in the interests of obtaining more correct and therefore fairer decisions. Many of these are probably Australian, as their team seem to have a penchant for burning their reviews and then suffering poor decisions which cost them a match or even a series. (Think Chandimal's edge during his series-levelling double century at Galle in 2022, and of course Stokes' non-LBW to Lyon at the very end of his Headingley 2019 epic – though in this case the resulting tied series still left Australia retaining the Ashes, always the prime focus of cricket's oldest international rivalry.)

For myself, I would find this just a little too dehumanising for the game. Would we like to have two umpires out there, merely calling the end of each over and each session and monitoring the players' conduct and occasional 'spirit of cricket' issues , while leaving every decision to invisible officials sitting in front of an array of TV screens in the pavilion? Then why should they even do that? A robot on the field or computer off it could just as well activate a bell or siren after every six balls.

Umpires have survived all the upheavals in cricket and are still playing essentially the same role as they did more than two centuries ago. The off-field officials and the technological aids are a very useful adjunct to ensure more accurate decisions. But the two umpires on the field remain what they have always been:

a necessary, venerated and beloved part of the game. Their role may be reduced if proponents of the above viewpoint have their way at the ICC. But they will always be there. Cricket is like a rugby union team: it needs fifteen people on the field.

## 18. FIXERS AND FIXING FIXED
*(Curbing collusion and corruption in the game)*

"Say it ain't so, Joe!" The child fan looked at the renowned batting star, whom he'd recognised instantly in the street, with pleading eyes. The star batter could only reply sadly, "I'm afraid it is, son." The boy burst into tears.

Though infinitely far from ever being a renowned batting star in any code, I can relate exactly to the way 'Shoeless' Joe Jackson felt when a young fan asked him whether some of his teammates in the Chicago Red Sox – dubbed the 'Black Sox' by the press in the wake of the scandal – had really accepted bribes to lose the 1919 World Series. (For those with zero interest in baseball, this was like one team throwing the final of the cricket, FIFA or rugby union World Cup. 'Shoeless' got his moniker because his parents were too dirt-poor to buy him footwear when he first went to baseball practices.)

"Say it ain't so" was more or less the plea of my then fourteen-year-old nephew one morning in 2000 when he phoned to ask me whether the reports about Hansie Cronje being fingered for match-fixing were true; and of course my answer was much the same as Shoeless Joe's. Countless other dads and uncles were doubtless answering the same question with equal sadness. The Proteas captain had always been seen as a role model, clean-living and well-mannered; but now, for the young fans who adored him – and many older ones – the idol had proved to have feet of clay.

The main point about Cronje's fall from grace, in the long run, was the degree of Richard Nixon-like forgiveness and redemption that he was granted – a process intensified, naturally, by his tragic early death only two years after his disgrace. I saw a burly fan at Centurion soon after Cronje's death carrying a large cut-out poster of the fallen hero with the caption "SALUEER SIR HANSIE" (Salute Sir Hansie). Other spectators expressed their approval, while I mused on the idea of Sir Wessel Johan Cronje as South Africa's first and only cricket knight.

Cronje, of course, was caught up in a trend in cricket that became a scourge towards the turn of the millennium, along with other SA players (notably Herschelle Gibbs, of whom more shortly.) During this period I personally witnessed two utterly contrasting cases of match-fixing: one was not suspected by anybody at first, while the other was fairly obvious but never acknowledged, even to this day.

I was at that infamous fifth day of the Fifth Test at Centurion in 2000 when three days had been lost to rain and not even one innings completed. Test history's only forfeited innings and only effective one-innings match occurred after Cronje and England's Nasser Hussain agreed to 'play a game', as Hussain later put it in his autobiography. It is highly unlikely that these landmarks will ever be repeated by any other Test captains, given the fallout.

What is forgotten today is that most people, except the strongest purist traditionalists, thought at the time that it was a good idea, an enterprising initiative, given that the series had already been settled with South Africa leading 2-0. Even the neutral Australian press asked "Who loses?" The answer, of course, turned out to be Test cricket's reputation, as it emerged that Cronje had accepted a leather jacket from a bookmaker to ensure there was a positive result (the bookie was South African, it will be recalled, destroying the argument that Cronje's only sin had been to talk naively to the wrong people on another continent).

The other case was far more sinister and secretive. I was watching a World Cup match on TV with other enthusiasts, when we began to smell a rat. Not once, but twice, batters stopped, changed direction and almost ran to the same end in obvious and successful efforts to get one of them run out. It would have been comical had it not been for the implications. Somebody said with almost a sense of wonder, using a then popular term for fixing, "I've never seen a cooked cricket match before." I won't mention the teams involved or the date even now. The popular SA administrator Ali Bacher, according to his biography, dared to mention the incident at an ICC meeting some years later as though it were an accepted if unacknowledged fact that the match had been fixed. Bacher received a severe rebuke, especially from the country that won on the day.

One ludicrous episode in an unfunny saga involved another South African, the highly talented but trouble-prone opener Herschelle Gibbs. Reports on the King Commission into alleged corruption in SA cricket suggested that Gibbs had once promised a bookmaker to get out cheaply in an ODI, but then scored a rapid 80 or so that proved to be match-winning. Gibbs apparently passed up the chance to claim he'd had a noble change of heart, instead saying he'd simply forgotten about the bookmaker in the heat of battle. Presumably he was never paid out nor approached by the bookie again, so it all ended well.

Today virtually all such match-rigging has been wiped out

by cricket's dedicated Anti-Corruption Commission, backed by the threats of suspensions, life bans and even jail sentences. Three-month prison terms were famously imposed on three Pakistani cricketers by a British court in 2011 for the apparently lesser crime of 'spot-fixing' (the judge ruled that those blessed with special talents also had special responsibilities to set good moral examples – a precept that all the fathers who had to explain Hansie Cronje's conduct to their sons would have heartily endorsed).

Betting, of course, remains a vibrant and acceptable part of cricket, as long as there is not the slightest hint of collusion with the players. Anything like the 500-1 bet that Dennis Lillee and Rod Marsh placed against their own side during Botham's Ashes of 1981 is as inconceivable in today's climate as the Cronje-Hussain deal. But there are few of us who have never looked at the odds being offered on the respective sides, especially during a tense clash. The same applies to most other sports. A Tongan rugby international even changed his name to Paddy Power. One wonders whether he runs the Irish bookmaker's local franchise in the South Pacific.

# D. ABOUT ALL-ROUNDERS

*(All-rounders have always intrigued me: the versatile multi-skillers of the game, the players for all seasons, the Renaissance men and women. Determining the best and greatest among them can be and has been done by careful statistical analysis. Here I am giving a more subjective account of the most outstanding all-rounders, based on impressions and reputation as much as figures, as well as some personal criteria.)*

# 19. THE UBER-ALL-ROUNDERS
## (*aka the 7-D Players*)

It's always seemed to me that the very best 'all-rounders' are those who can do more than just bat and bowl up to international standard; they can do both disciplines in several different ways, covering almost the full spectrum of cricket skills. Cricinfo had an intriguing debate on the point in late 2021, mostly based on intricate analysis and weighting of statistics. In contrast, I've looked for far more abstract qualities in choosing what I call the 'uber-all-rounders'. I look for seven different dimensions – six playing skills and one quality going beyond cricket – so I'll call them 7-D players. They have to possess most or all of the six playing skills, naturally at the highest international levels. The six skills are:

(i) Top order batting in Tests, implying the patience and ability to build a long innings as well as the skill;

(ii) 'Power hitting', especially the ability to be a 'finisher' or 'enforcer' in white-ball games, as well as when required in red-ball;

(iii) Fast or fast-medium bowling good enough to take the new ball at Test or other international level;

(iv) Finger spinning at the highest level;

(v) Wrist spinning likewise;

(vi) Captaincy: leading a team with competence, success and

the respect of their teams. (I don't include fielding, as most players with a skills set like the above seem to generally field first slip and do it superbly).

(vii) To these I add a seventh quality that I will call 'charisma'. The 7-D player must be a character, an outstanding personality, a figure who is known, liked, respected and admired even beyond cricket.

A tall order. Allowing very slight latitude, I have found only three players who qualify. One is obvious, Sir Garfield Sobers, and another predictable, Keith Miller. The third may be a surprise: Michael Procter. Because he played only seven Tests, Mike Procter is often not included in statistical lists and even full-length books on the best all-rounders. Yet his first-class career was superlative. I'm not biased in his favour because he is South African, except in that this is the reason he played so few Tests. He was fully appreciated at the English county he played for, Gloucestershire – his role was so great that the county was sometimes jokingly called 'Proctershire' – and a stand at their home ground is named after him. Because so much has already been written about the three players, I won't deal with each one in turn, but rather focus on the seven dimensions, or criteria, that I've set out above. The three players' best-known feats, mentioned here, were of course representative of many others:

*Top-order red-ball batting*: Sobers held the record for the highest Test innings, 365, for thirty-seven years. Enough said, without reference to his many other remarkable Test innings. Miller batted as high as 3 or 4 for Australia, especially earlier in his career, and was able to curb his natural aggressive instincts when the match situation demanded it. Procter is bracketed with no less than Donald Bradman and C.B. Fry in scoring six consecutive first-class centuries. It was true that this was achieved in the B Section of South Africa's domestic Currie Cup; but some of the bowlers he had to face were useful, and he still had to find the application and consistency to make the runs match after match. (I watched one of these centuries, in Pretoria some fifty km from where I then lived; people would travel a long way to watch Procter bat for Rhodesia during that season.)

*Power hitting:* Sobers was the first to hit six sixes in an over, happily captured on TV for posterity. Miller regularly hit enormous blows, mainly slog-sweeps, especially in the 'Victory Tests' just after World War II. Procter went just short of Sobers when he once smashed the Australian off-spinner Ashley Mallett for five sixes in an over for Western Province in Cape Town.

*Fast or fast-medium bowling*: Sobers was a skilful left-arm fast-medium bowler who sometimes took the new ball for the West Indies. Miller and Procter are both acknowledged to have been among the very best of the genuinely fast bowlers.

*Finger spinning*: Sobers was so versatile that he was first picked for the Windies as a left-arm spinner. Miller could and did bowl whole spells of off-spin, notably in 'Laker's Test' when the Old Trafford pitch obviously suited that type of bowling. Procter could bowl devastating off-breaks (with a normal action that followed a very brief Shane Warne-like amble to the stumps); his only 'niner' in an innings (9-71) was achieved not by pace, but with off-spin that dismantled a strong Transvaal batting line-up on a turner in Bulawayo.

*Wrist spinning*: Sobers later turned in his slower mode to what were then called 'chinamen' with great effect. Miller was known for steaming in off his full run-up and then bowling a perfectly pitched googly (or conversely coming in off two steps to deliver a vicious bouncer). I saw Procter vary his off-spin with a leg-break now and again, with no loss of control.

*Captaincy*: Sobers captained Windies well enough for a long period, though he once lost a series with a generous declaration that allowed Boycott, of all batters, to anchor a successful England run chase against the clock. Miller was vice-captain of Australia and a legendary leader of New South Wales: a later national captain, Bob Simpson, describes his debut state match in which Miller, placing his field, told him, "And you, young Simpson, beat it to fine leg' or words to that effect", the exact words being easy enough to guess. Procter was a much-respected captain at some stage of almost every team he played for, including 'South Africa' at the start of the unrecognised rebel tours.

*Charisma*: Sir Gary was duly knighted, though his popularity came not just from his services to cricket but an almost incredible modesty for a player of his stature. He took a great interest in South Africa after the end of isolation and visited the country a few times, mainly to look at developing players. During one of these trips, a local cricket reporter described him as just 'the former West Indies captain', clearly being too new at his job to know about Sobers the legend; Sobers of course had said nothing to enlighten the young reporter.

Miller could and should have had a film made about his life, perhaps starring as himself with his 'Cavalier-in-a Roundhead-world' looks. I will suggest just three scenes for the movie, based on: (i) Miller's wartime service as a fighter pilot, leading to his comment that real pressure wasn't Test cricket but "having a Messerschmitt up your arse", (ii) his famous friendship with Denis Compton, both reportedly sipping champagne while other cricketers swilled their beer, which is still honoured with the Compton-Miller award for the best player in each Ashes series; and (iii) his less famous friendship with Princess Margaret, which would have made ideal material for an episode of *The Crown* if the producers of that mostly fictional royal soap opera had done a little more homework.

Procter has always been 'Procky', an admired, respected and loved figure wherever he called home, whether his native Natal, Gloucestershire, Western Province or the former Rhodesia. He became equally respected as an elder statesman of the game after retirement. His work as an ICC Match Referee is remembered for two controversies that were very hard to deal with (the Pakistan forfeiture and the Harbajhan Singh/Andrew Symonds affair) – an unlucky chance, as the Match Referee can usually just sit back and enjoy the Test in ninety-nine games out of a hundred. We'll see more of Procter in other Bites.

But there is so much more about cricket's multi-skillers and so many more players to mention. The traditional definition is still valid: an all-rounder is a player who would get into the side for *either* his batting alone or his bowling alone. I want to highlight a number of them in the next Bite.

# 20. MORE ON ALL-ROUNDERS

*(Here I talk first about three noted English all-rounders, one contemporary as I write, whose names seem to belong together. Next, I go to a decade that saw as many as five indisputably great all-rounders all playing roughly at the same time, for whatever reason. Last comes a look at today's versatile players in an age of increasing specialisation.)*

**A. England's Talismanic Trio**

Three English all-rounders of the last three generations are very often mentioned in the same breath. **Sir Ian Botham, Andrew 'Freddie' Flintoff** and **Ben Stokes** are often seen as making up a kind of glorious (mostly) line of succession. Consider the points in common: all three powerful batters, able to hit fiercely and far when required; all three fast-medium bowlers who seemed genuinely fast at times, all three reluctant to part with the ball when in the mood; all three regarded as talismans of England during their respective periods. Botham and Flintoff could and did run through any team in their more inspired moments; Stokes as a bowler perhaps falls a little short of their heights, having perhaps never recovered from that match-winning assault of four sixes that Carlos Brathwaite inflicted on him in the 2016 T20 World Cup final. Botham won the 1981 Ashes close to single-handedly; Flintoff had a huge role in the shock 2005 Ashes victory; and Stokes' batting with its penchant for the big occasion had, at time of writing, squared and Ashes and won a 50-over World Cup (both 2019) as well as the 20-over version (2022).

Do you make your kingpin all-rounder the captain, adding to his burden? England tried it with Botham and Flintoff, experiments that didn't succeed. Stokes, however, is poles apart from the others in this respect. Appointed in 2022 to turn around England's fortunes, he has done that in spades or higher. Stokes has been able to bring his charisma and determination to the captaincy, with a kind of Midas touch in most of what he does as captain. He has turned England's fortunes around at the time of writing, with victories against New Zealand, India and South Africa at home in 2022 and Pakistan away, using a new and startling approach (see **Bite 27 for a 2023 update**). Stokes has acquired the aura of a St George-King Arthur-James Bond kind of English action hero, slaying opposition dragons to drag England from disasters to triumphs. And he seems to actually find the job of being England captain fun, whereas his predecessors always seemed grim-faced – at least since David Gower or perhaps even the always smiling A.P.F. Chapman a century ago.

The Talismanic Trio could be described, either from their last initials or their nicknames Beefy, Freddie and Stokesey, as the BFS players. It happens that the letters follow in alphabetical order. Perhaps England's selectors should watch out, come 2030 or so, for a young all-rounder who has outstanding talents and a final initial between T and Z.

### B. The decade of the Big Five all-rounders

Sir Ian Botham is the overlap between the BFS and another notable group of all-rounders. The decade of the 1980s saw four – or, arguably, five – outstanding all-rounders all playing at the same time. These were Botham, Kapil Dev, Imran Khan and Sir

Richard Hadlee (whose batting fell a little short of the others, but not by much). It's hard to analyse why this happened: perhaps it had something to do with the growth of one-day cricket. The South African Clive Rice was contemporary with these four and can arguably be rated alongside them, as I suggest in the next Bite. In 1987, I managed to see four of these five all-round giants playing in the same match, the MCC vs Rest of the World fiesta described in **Bite 46**.

**C. All-rounders today:**

There are, in a sense, far more all-rounders about now than there ever were, thanks to the demands of white-ball cricket. Most bowlers are now able to bat a bit because they have to: runs are often needed from the tail in the latter stages of a 50 or even a 20-over innings. This has rubbed off on the long format, where it's becoming increasingly common for tail-enders to come to light with the bat and sometimes change the whole course of a Test. It is no longer a surprise for a side's last five wickets to add more than the first five. Frontline bowlers like Pat Cummins and R. Ashwin have turned themselves into all-rounders. Conversely, more batters bowl a bit now because they're needed: team selections for the limited formats sometimes require the captain to divide up the fifth bowler's quota among these batters who can bowl. Again this has rubbed off on Test cricket: more specialist batters are succeeding with the red ball, the prime current example perhaps being Joe Root.

Even the kind of multi-dimensional skill sets seen in the '7-D players' are less rare than they were – though not to the extent that Sobers, Miller and Procter possessed them (see **Bite 19**) – and in bowling, this is thanks to the growth of T20 play in particular. In the desperate bid to contain batters whose sole mission in the death overs is to score as many runs as possible, bowlers have to resort to every variation of pace and movement they can muster. This in turn has caused the quicker bowlers not merely to develop slower balls but to learn how to make them deviate in one direction or the other by spin or cut.

Cricket remains a game of 'glorious uncertainty'. The old Victorian cliché is meant to apply to the progress of a particular match, but it is equally true of broader developments, specifically the emergence of new players. Today's game needs and encourages outstanding all-rounders. There is no reason why a new Botham, Kallis, Procter or Miller should not surface at any time in any of the major cricket countries (or a minor country, but then he would probably be poached). A new Sobers is not impossible. We should, or rather could, be so lucky.

# 21. THE UNLUCKIEST PLAYER EVER
## *("Rice! Rice! Rice!")*

The chant of the local hero's name echoed around the Wanderers as if the stadium had been hosting a schools athletics meeting. But it came from mainly adult spectators, and not once but regularly. Every delivery by Clive Rice at this time was fraught with expectation. Players still wore long-sleeved shirts, and for some reason Rice rolled up the sleeve of his bowling (right) arm with his left hand as he walked back for every delivery. It seemed a compulsive habit, perhaps a ritual like a batter tapping his bat. Whatever the case, once Rice turned and started to run in, it was all action. The crowd chanted the bowler's name, climaxing as he released the ball. The batter needed to be in a tight 'bubble' not to be affected. (I'd read of Australian crowds chanting "Lillee! Lillee!" in such a way that it almost sounded like "Kill! Kill!" The Wanderers crowd supporting Rice were a little less ferocious.)

This was when Rice was at his peak as a player, helping Transvaal (the forerunner of today's Lions) ride roughshod over strong provincial opposition. In his golden season of 1979/80, hardly a match went by without him making significant runs or taking several wickets, often both. As a bowler he probably ranged between genuinely fast and fast-medium, but certainly found devastating bounce and movement on greentops that were undeniably prepared largely for Rice and his fellow quicks. Opponents called the Wanderers 'the Bullring' and the pitches 'snakepits'. The least successful matadors/snake handlers were Eastern Province, in a match which I watched for all one-and-a-half days it lasted. EP were all out for 86 and 46 with two men retired hurt, mostly through Rice's agency. As a batter he curiously made his maiden first-class century only in this season, after ten years as a leading all-rounder and a good many 90's, Trevor Goddard-like. I was watching when he finally reached the mark against the one team that could give Transvaal a run for their money, Western Province. He crossed his arms above his head, like a victorious boxer apart from the bat in one hand – which seemed just then like a mace for battering the foe.

That season, practically mid-career for Rice, was a hard act to follow. But he kept up very high all-round standards with Nottinghamshire and Transvaal for a further decade and more. With his forceful character, it was natural that he soon captained both the county and the province, as well as the unofficial SA XI in the rebel tour era. He was South Africa's Mr Cricket in at least two senses: as the first name that came to mind when you mentioned cricket, and for his meticulous Michael Hussey-like attitude to the game. I heard Rice speak a few times, and his commonest phrases were always "attention to detail" and "refining my technique." One sign of this was that he was among the first batters to take his stance with his bat raised off the ground.

He demanded respect and was as ready to give it. My two clearest non-playing images of him are contrasting. One is known to everyone in cricket, when he humbly greeted Mother Teresa with clasped hands during that historic 1991 tour of India. The other is known only to members of the SA Cricket Society: asked as guest speaker for his thoughts about Notts's rich history, he told us one of his proudest moments was being photographed with an aged Larwood and Voce as the current county captain at the renaming of the gates at Trent Bridge after the county's great pace duo.

Rice was very forthright, told people when he didn't agree with them and did things his way. The cheeky advertisement in which he posed wearing only a well-placed bat (see **Bite 4**), did not endear him to the cricket establishment. His trademark Mexican-rebel 'droopy' moustache, sustained long after it went out of fashion, spoke of determination as well as defiance, a cricketing Zapata if you like. His differences with the SA selectors were probably what cost him any further place in the new official national team after he had been the automatic choice as captain for the ice-breaking 1991 tour of India. His age was cited; this was nonsense, as room was found for two other veterans, Peter Kirsten in the World Cup that followed and Jimmy Cook for two Test series soon afterwards.

The 1980s, the second decade of Rice's career, happened to see four great all-rounders flourishing at the same time, as noticed in the last Bite: Botham, Hadlee, Imran Khan and Kapil Dev. I believe that Rice deserves to be bracketed with them as a 'Big Five'. (The presence of so many great all-rounders together prompted the tobacco-makers Silk Cut – acceptable sponsors then – to hold single-wicket tournaments to which the top all-rounders were invited. Not much can be read into the results of such a gimmicky enterprise; yet the fact remains that Rice won three out of the four Silk Cut competitions that were played. Perhaps, as the only one of the 'Big Five' who wasn't playing international cricket, he had a point to prove and was more motivated than the others by such an unimportant challenge.)

Rice's early death was sad; but in truth, South African cricket had made little use of his abilities and enormous insight into the game since his retirement as a player. A doer rather than a talker, he never wrote an autobiography. It was a pity that nobody ever wrote his biography.

The Unluckiest Player Ever? Well, the pinnacle of any player's career is still presumably representing his or her country in international matches in one or more of the formats (I would like to think that playing in Tests is still the ultimate goal for players, though financial factors obviously influence their career decisions). Clive Rice's career coincided very closely with South Africa's isolation. He was selected for the 1970 tour of England that never happened; twenty-one years later he played his only three official international matches, that ODI series against India. So I regard him as the game's unluckiest player. Similarly, I'd argue that there is a strong case for judging C.E.B. Rice to be the best cricketer never to have won a Test cap.

# E. SUPREMOS SEEN LIVE (or not)

*(The august all-rounders just discussed generally fell short of the very highest echelon of batters and bowlers, though some came very close. Three players who were in that echelon – judged by any yardstick – performed in South Africa in recent decades. So, rather than add to the reams already written about the three, I offer fresh perspectives on their exploits and reception in SA, many of which I watched live. The best batter of all time – by irrefutable figures – never came to the country. In much lighter vein, I look at the way his name was bandied about in SA.)*

## 22. SACHIN IN SOUTH AFRICA
### *(The Maestro's Milestone)*

Sachin Tendulkar may be the best batter ever seen in South Africa, if you agree with the widespread opinion that he was the second best ever (SA missed out on seeing Bradman on the 1935/36 tour; he sat it out following a life-threatening illness, not that Australia needed him in that series.) Tendulkar is possibly as much of an icon as Bradman, given the enormous passion for the game in India. South Africa was fortunate enough to see him on five tours between 1992 and 2010: he made at least one century on all but one of them. Such stats probably apply to Sachin in most Test countries over his long and superlative career. But he also made a more intangible impact in SA, as I'll try to explain.

What I really noted about Sachin in South Africa was his reception by the local fans. The Saffers, very often given to patriotic one-sided spectatorship (I won't attempt comparisons with other nations) always accorded him a special respect that was rarely granted to any opponent. There was not just warm applause but loud cheering when he walked in, struck his many boundaries, reached his many landmarks and when he departed. Very unlike a South African crowd, a silence would sometimes descend on the ground when he was batting as fans waited for the next piece of artistry. Once when Donald famously castled Tendulkar and celebrated with an airliner impression (quickly used in an ad by SA Airways), there was of course jubilation in the home crowd. But even that was clearly a compliment to the status of the batter dismissed, and the wild cheers for Donald channelled seamlessly into appreciation of Tendulkar as he left. In my mind's eye, I imagined Bradman being received like that in South Africa if he'd ever come.

Much could be written, but here are just two instances of Sachin supremacy in SA that are still remembered. The first happened at Newlands, with Table Mountain providing a suitably majestic backdrop. In the New Year Test in 1996, Tendulkar and Azharuddin shared what was acknowledged as one of the best partnerships ever seen in South Africa, coming together with India on 58/5 and adding 222. Rather than attempting a technical analysis – you know how they both batted – I'll mention the comparison that was made at the time locally. During the Durban Test of 1970, Barry Richards (140) and Graeme Pollock (274) were together for just one hour of the home side's long first innings, after lunch on the first day. About 100 runs were scored in that hour: those lucky enough to watch it (no TV in SA then) said it was all just real glorious cricket strokes, never a hint of slogging or haste. The Tendulkar-Azharuddin partnership was immediately compared by commentators with that one, which, for any South African fan, was the highest praise.

Tendulkar went on after Azhar's dismissal, though with too little support left to change the course of the match. He was last out for 169, and then only to a piece of brilliance worthy of his innings. Adam Bacher (Ali's nephew) hauled in a strong aerial pull to a long midwicket boundary with an extraordinary sprinting, diving one-handed catch. Sachin's reaction was memorable. Rather than taking a run, he stood with hands on hips watching the catch with amazement that turned to admiration – you could see it all in his expression. Then he walked back, with the applause for Bacher's catch (as with the Donald dismissal) seguing smoothly into appreciation of his innings.

The other instance was of unique statistical significance. Only once has a player ever reached his fiftieth Test century, and I was lucky enough to be at Centurion's Supersport Park in late 2010 to see the moment. It should have happened at his home ground, Mumbai's Wankhede Stadium or at least in India; I felt at the time for all the devoted Indian fans watching on TV who would have loved to be sitting where I was. The match had already seen a less imposing landmark: Jacques Kallis, who after fourteen years of excellence had never made a Test double century, finally reached the mark, with Smith delaying his declaration to let him do it. Kallis piled up his runs alongside de Villiers and Amla; it was something to see these three batters making centuries in the same innings (I think this may have been the only time), but the pitch was playing too well and the match too one-sided for this to seem so very memorable. I think I can say the Saffer fans mostly perceived that the biggest milestone was still to come (admittedly it helped that the home side was almost certain of victory, so patriotic inclinations were already assuaged).

The ground was just as full as before on the fourth day for the bulk of India's second innings, as they tried to make inroads on a deficit of almost 500. The talk now was all about the Little Maestro's fiftieth Test century. Sachin was at centre stage in a way that far transcended the context of the match, last seen during Lara's progress to 400 in Antigua six years earlier. I think it was fair to say the fans had come to see the milestone as much as a home victory.

It all went according to script, but that didn't detract in the least from the occasion. Tendulkar played his normal magnificent game as the wickets fell. He watched unruffled as

Dhoni, captaining the side, thrashed an ODI-style 90, but didn't bother to join the fun. Sachin reached his milestone shortly before stumps and the crowd erupted, giving him the best ovation conceivable outside India. He even went on to add a fifty-first Test century, another one at Newlands, in the last match of the series. It was a fitting farewell to a country where he had given immense pleasure over eighteen years.

Reviewing this Bite, I realise that on every occasion I've singled out, Tendulkar shared his glory with others. It doesn't matter: what he did easily outshone the concurrent feats of Donald, Azhar, Bacher and Kallis. South African fans appreciated and properly honoured the greatness of the Little Maestro.

## 23. SHANE IN SOUTH AFRICA
### (*Thirteen years of batting guesswork*)

*"Nou verstaan hulle meer van Warne se boulwerk as die hele Proteas-kolflys.*" An Afrikaans newspaper once commented that a group of schoolboys in one of South Africa's less privileged areas now understood more about Shane Warne's bowling arts than the entire Proteas batting line-up. This was after Warne gave a coaching clinic in the area. For some reason the great leg-spinner, arguably the Greatest Of All Time (or GOAT, as it's irreverently abbreviated today) decided to show off all his trade secrets in this unlikely setting. Bemused schoolboys and astonished reporters watched the master showing off his art. Out came two types of leg-break, the flipper, the slider, the 'zooter' and all. (I can't remember if the report mentioned a googly, which would have cost Warne a sharp pain after his shoulder injury.)

    The point of the sarcastic dig at the Proteas batters was, of course, that none of them was ever able to read Warne consistently throughout the four tours he made of SA from 1993/4 to 2005/6, let alone the four series in Australia over those years. It was not that he ran through the home line-up, as he often did to home teams in other countries; pitches in South Africa are generally not spinner-friendly enough for even Warne (or Muralidharan) to do that. Instead, the twelve home Test matches almost all saw the SA batters involved in long contests of fierce concentration and grim guesswork against Warne, playing him mostly from the pitch. With little idea from the bowler's hand what the ball was going to do, they tried to preserve their wickets and picked up runs where they could. He held them in thrall even when he wasn't dismissing them. Warne didn't get many five-fors in South Africa. But typically he would take three-for or four-for, while McGrath and the other seamers did the rest. SA never had enough runs and won only a single Test apart from 'dead rubbers' in all those four series. The only time in those series that the home batters passed 400, threatening to build up a winning lead – in the second innings on a placid Newlands pitch in 2002 – Warne wheeled down 70 overs and took 6-161 to keep them in check so that Australia needed 331, which on the still easy track proved quite gettable.

The uneasiness SA batters felt with Warne – even Hansie Cronje couldn't bring off his famed slog-sweep against him very often – translated into a deep respect, and with it, an understanding of the man's quirks. When Warne gave the opener Andrew Hudson a curse-laden send-off that was unacceptable at any level of the game, Hudson looked astonished rather than angry. Hudson later laughed it off as 'white-line fever' and readily accepted Warne's apology, which Warne even repeated in his autobiography. Daryll Cullinan suffered the indignity, for a world-class batter, of becoming Warne's 'bunny', but could still indulge in good-natured banter directed at his tormentor's growing girth in a famous exchange: "I've been waiting for three years to bowl to you again." "Yes, and you look as if you've spent it eating pizzas and ice-cream." And Jonty Rhodes forged a very close friendship with Warne, based on their shared passion and gusto for the game. This led to private visits to South Africa in aid of cricket development, including coaching clinics such as the one mentioned. (The clinics never threw up a home-grown

SA leg-spinner of Test calibre, but this simply does not exist as a local species, as discussed in **Bite 35**.)

South Africans were not only as dumbfounded as the rest of the cricket world at Shane Warne's stunning death in March 2022, but also felt they had lost a friend as well as an iconic rival. The collective sigh of relief among opposing teams when he retired in 2007 was blown away by the global gasp of anguish when he died a scant fifteen years later – and these reactions were nowhere more pronounced than in South Africa.

*(Some will question why Muttiah Muralidharan's performances in South Africa are not also discussed here. The short answer is that he did not have the same mesmerising effect on the home batters on SA pitches as Warne, though they generally played him with the great care due to his unremitting accuracy and only occasionally attacked him with the slog-sweep.)*

## 24. BRIAN CHARLES IN SOUTH AFRICA
### *(The best to watch?)*

One other name deserves mention in this company. Brian Charles Lara – he was one of those players whose full names seemed to have a far better ring – fell short of his contemporary Tendulkar in terms of numbers (even though Lara scored 375, 400 and 501 where Tendulkar never reached 250). But Lara is regularly rated above SRT in terms of less definable qualities: grace, style, beauty. Even music was often invoked in writers' effort to describe his batting. In a respectful bow to this abstract status, I'll look briefly at his two tours of South Africa, on both of which he captained West Indies.

The first tour, in 1998/99, was forgettable, and frankly a disappointment after the long decades that SA fans had waited to see the storied islanders, their appetites whetted by some visits by Sir Garfield Sobers after re-admission to world cricket. The Windies team almost didn't come, thanks to a players' strike (led by Lara) and when they did, looked distracted and listless. They were blanked 5-0, with Lara managing only three fifties, showing mere glimpses of his class.

But B.C. Lara did leave an indelible impression during his second visit in 2003/4. Over four Tests, Lara made a double century, a century and a 70 that exuded elegance and class. The 202 at the Wanderers, out of a team total of only 410, was a masterpiece that gave South Africans a hint of those famous innings – the 153, 277, 375, 400 and 501, among others – that they'd read of him playing in other arenas. The 202 contained a gem within a gem, when the mostly outgunned Windies needed 29 to avoid the follow-on and, with only three tail-enders and an injured Chris Gayle for company, Lara seemed to fear he would run out of partners first. He quite suddenly switched tempo and set on the left-arm spinner Robin Peterson, wiping off 28 of these runs from one over. There was nothing savage or brutal about it: when Peterson pitched it up, Lara simply advanced and used smooth swings of the bat to propel each ball at frightening speed straight or to long-on, and when Peterson dropped it short, Lara effortlessly checked his advance, switched his weight and played an exquisite late cut. Peterson looked on in rueful but awed admiration; the Wanderers fans were in raptures. They knew they'd been granted a window onto the ability of a player who, on other continents and against other bowlers (Warne and Glen McGrath included), had proved himself peerless in his own way.

## 25. SOUTH AFRICAN BRADMAN?
### *(There hasn't been one, but it's fun to look at the comparisons)*

Fascinating pub topic though it is, nobody, however clued-up on sport, will ever be able to prove definitively that Messi was better than Pele, Federer or Djokovic than Laver, Tiger Woods than Ben Hogan, Springbok lock Victor Matfield than the legendary Frik du Preez – you get the drift. The variables between sporting generations are just too great to make meaningful comparisons in most sports; even the statistics, apparently an objective basis, do not provide conclusive arguments.

With cricket – where statistics count for more than in most sports in any case – it is different. Donald Bradman is so *facile princeps,* so easily first, with his famous 99.94 Test batting average more than 20 points ahead of the next best, that very few seriously dispute the Australian's claim to be 'the greatest cricketer of all time'. Hardly anybody even raises the argument that cricket includes three disciplines and that a player who was a master only of batting, should therefore not be given the supreme rating. The Bradman argument is rather: will there ever be, could there be, has there been, another Bradman?

My aim here is not to open a fruitless debate based on factors other than the plain statistics, but rather to ponder very briefly whether South Africa has ever had anyone coming close to the

Don. The short answer is no: Barry Richards and AB de Villiers perhaps come the nearest, but an enormous gap still separates them, like every other master batter, from Bradman. In lighter vein, it's amusing to look at the two instances I'm aware of when the South African and other media actually dared to mention a local player in the same breath as Bradman.

Ali Bacher, better remembered today for administration and captaincy, was a good enough batter to hold down a Test top-order spot, but never rivalled the legends Richards and Graeme Pollock in the side he captained. Yet when he first emerged as a batter of note, Bacher was hailed as the new Bradman by a transplanted Australian journalist of all critics. Richard 'Dick' Whitington even went as far as saying Bacher was better than the two Australians who had also been proclaimed the new Bradman by their own media, Ian Craig and Norman O'Neill. Whitington was a cricket writer prone to exaggeration and fond of stirring the pot; but then the far more staid South African Cricket Annual, the local Wisden if you like, endorsed his judgment by comparing Bacher with Bradman while naming him a Cricketer of the Year.

Bacher, in Rodney Hartman's biography, has admitted that this became something of a millstone around his neck, as it would be for any player. What made it worse was that since childhood he had read everything he could about the great man and kept Bradman's *The Art of Cricket* always on hand as a virtual bible of the game. Bacher would face bigger problems in his career, especially as an administrator, but his regard for *The Art of Cricket* remained so high that he presented copies to the two most successful post-isolation SA captains, Hansie Cronje and Graeme Smith.

Which brings me to Smith and Bradman; this, fortunately for

Smith, was never a serious comparison like the Bacher millstone, but merely a statistical achievement and a clever headline. Smith stunned the cricket world by making Bradmanesque scores of 277 and 259 in his first full series as a stripling twenty-three-year-old captain touring England in 2003. The latter score, as it happened, broke a Bradman record that had stood for seventy-three years, for the highest score by a foreign player at Lord's (this was Bradman's 254 in 1930, often rated his best innings). A Johannesburg newspaper cleverly invoked a then recent movie title with its headline on Smith's achievement: "Belt it like Bradman" (in case anyone has forgotten, the hit film *Bend it like Beckham* paid tribute to David Beckham's banana-curving free kicks, reminiscent of in- or out-swingers at cricket, while incidentally also introducing the charms of Keira Knightley to the world). Smith, who never quite achieved such levels again in an overall excellent career, probably enjoyed the headline as much as anybody if he ever saw it.

There will surely never be another Bradman, from South Africa or any other country. The pressures of the modern game, playing almost continuously for eleven to twelve months a year across all three formats (what would an IPL franchise bid for such a batter?), would make it almost impossible. So, probably, would the constant video analysis by coaches or opponents looking for the slightest flaw in his technique: no doubt they would come up with a more subtle and sustainable tactic than England's relatively successful Body-line counter to the original Bradman (who managed to average 'only' 54 for Body-line's only series before the tactic was outlawed).

Yet the bar he set is remains a summit for players to aim at, the gold standard for batters. As memories of the actual player fade into a kind of semi-legendary mist, the cricket media will be less likely to bandy such comparisons – a mercy for players like Bacher who were only hindered by them. And if the comparison were made, the affected player could always look at the YouTube of Bradman's final Test innings as cricket's ultimate symbol of the fallibility of icons and the levelling power of sport.

# F. WOMEN'S CRICKET

# 26. LIBERTY, EQUALITY AND SORORITY
## *(Everything but the brute strength)*

I apologise again for any suggestion in these Bites that only men play cricket, including the use of masculine pronouns for generic cricketers and officials. I have to admit that I have only taken a real interest in women's cricket for a decade or so. However, I long ago noticed the change in the playing garb from the schoolgirl skirts and long socks of the past to today's uniformity with male teams' coloured white-ball garb. This is entirely in keeping with changes in society and men's far more respectful attitudes to women in sport. Even sport surfing now dresses its women competitors in T-shirts and board shorts, not the mandatory bikinis of an earlier era.

The women Proteas (who used South Africa's national flower as their emblem long before the men) have won the interest and respect of the most macho male Saffer fans by their consistent performances over the past few years while the men's team was often floundering. Their matches at the Women's World Cup in 2022 pushed domestic men's games firmly into the background. Laura Wolvaardt is firmly established among South Africa's leading sports stars. Sune Luus, Lizelle Lee, Mariska Kapp, Chloe Tryon, Ayabonga Khaka and others are as much household names now as their male counterparts. The all-conquering Australian women's team and some of their English and Indian counterparts are also well-known names. Questions about them are posed and correctly answered in pub quizzes – one of the surest signs of sporting recognition in South Africa, as elsewhere. And the collective groan of resignation when the South African women exited the tournament at England's hands, "There they go, losing in the semi-finals *again!*" implied a pleasing sense of equality, even assimilation, with their male counterparts. Similarly in the women's T20 World Cup in 2023, nobody hesitated to point out that a senior SA cricket team had made history by reaching a WC final for the first time.

A former member of the women Proteas (to name-drop a little) lived in the same townhouse estate in Johannesburg as me for some years. Sunette Viljoen (SA 2000-2002) would have gone further in cricket had she not been a world-class javelin thrower. She competed in four Olympic Games up to 2016 and would have it made it five had the Tokyo 2020 Games not been postponed to the following year. In cricket, Sunette's returns from the outfield must have been as powerful as most or all seen in the men's game.

In both real life and fiction, it has become quite common for a woman to take part in a match played mostly by men and give a good account of herself. Notable fictional examples include the Tillingfold stories of English village cricket as rebooted for the late twentieth century. We can even go as far back as the early 1800s with the film *Becoming Jane*. A young Jane Austen, before becoming a best-selling author, plays cricket with a group of men and faces an under-arm (correct for the time) but distinctly quick delivery, which she dispatches (with an understandably baseball-style shot by the American actress playing Jane, Anne Hathaway). In real life, a Johannesburg lawyer once told me how her daughter played regularly for her junior high school's cricket team. She was generally the only girl on either side, and would quickly disabuse the boys in the opposing team who assumed she would be an easy wicket and/or felt they should bowl gently to her. Many mothers around the cricket world could probably tell similar stories.

Today we tune into women's cricket, or go to watch it live, in order to see technical proficiency, elegance, tactical battles and almost every aspect we would expect to find in a men's game, except perhaps the brute force. That is how it should be. Many of us wish we had discovered this compelling side of the game much earlier than we did.

# G. CRICKET IN THE 2020s

## 27. ENGLAND's 'TEST REVOLUTION'?
### *(Format-Fudging, Fun or Flash in the Pan?)*

Whatever England did to Test cricket in 2022 is, on the one hand, still unfolding at the time of writing; and on the other, has already had been the subject of copious comment and analysis. Here I'll confine myself to a few more or less light-hearted comments, based on possible names and abbreviating initials for the new brand/style/approach/philosophy (other nouns would serve just as well).

The English Test Revolution, ETR? Serious cricket critics have described it this way. The trouble is that the English don't do revolutions, at least not the bloody and violent kind. (King Charles the First was beheaded, true; but that was later admitted as an error, and his current namesake is safe from any repeat of that 1649 upheaval. A change of kings just thirty-nine years later was so bloodless that it was called the Glorious Revolution; and the (first) Industrial Revolution was really a long and gradual process of applying a series of brilliant inventions from about three hundred to two hundred years ago.) So ETR won't quite do.

Neither will the obvious BB. In this I respect the views of the two men themselves, the architect and the chief exponent. Baz and Ben are both on record as saying they don't like the term Bazball. They insist, rightly, that their brainchild is perfectly serious Test cricket, just played with a different mindset, more aggressive and less shackled by old assumptions, and certainly not approaching anywhere n'ear baseball.

I'd suggest MSC, for McCullum/Stokes Chutzpah. The last delightful word sums up the sheer boldness, daring, audacity, brazen cheek of the new style. And the hint of a higher degree in science does justice to the complex process of calculation, deliberation, appraisal, planning and execution that underlies the apparently carefree exploits on the pitch.

England have shown flexibility in applying 'MSC'. We may as well have some more fun with the initials. On a flat pitch in Pakistan late in 2022, they successfully extended the new approach from fourth-innings chases to a first-innings 6-7 RR extravaganza – Match-Seizing Conditions. On a livelier pitch and against a threatening new bowler, they adjusted to almost normal Test cricket – Mystery Spinner Correction. But with a smallish target on an easier pitch to complete a clean sweep, they gave even him the Mystery Spinner Charge. (Abrar Ahmed, incidentally, seems to be a folded-finger spinner of the same type as two past Australians, Jack Iverson and John Gleeson, though I've yet to see the comparison made). Speaking of Australia, 'MSC' faced a daunting challenge in mid-2023, which we can expand into MJPSC, the Mitch-Josh-Pat-Scott Confrontation. It ended inconclusively.

Sceptics believe England will choose the wrong moment to play red-ball-with-white-ball and come badly unstuck, perhaps sooner rather than later. My own prediction is that the 'MSC' will eventually subside from the crest of the wave, but not too far, and will spread to other teams. We'll increasingly see run rates in Test matches regularly rising above 4 per over, a direction in which Australia in particular have long been moving anyway. Other facets of the Buccaneering Ben style of Test captaincy have been called in question simply because they resulted in two defeats (marginal as both were) – enforcing the follow-on at Wellington in 2023 and declaring short of 400 in an Ashes first innings at Edgbaston later that year. McCullum has said he doesn't mind losing at times in the interests of his 'freeing up' of Test cricket, and it seems unlikely that he or Stokes will change anything.

What can't be denied is that applying short-format batting in long-format matches has worked spectacularly so far. The brave new England, coming out of a trough, saw off four of its five strongest rivals in the course of 2022. The juggernaut was checked in 2023, but only partially, with a marginally shared series in New Zealand and then the closest Ashes series ever. 'MSC', judiciously applied as seen, still had a 13-4 win ratio at the time of writing.

What also cannot be denied is that it is highly entertaining, even exhilarating, to watch. There can have been few cricket fans, even diehard Test traditionalists, who were not watching every possible minute of England's Test matches by the end of 2022. Fans around the world were glued to their screens for the 2023 Ashes series and in England, tickets for all five Test matches were like gold dust. BenBaz's England have shown that Test cricket can be fun; and their approach has proved to be much more than a flash in the pan.

# 28. THE SPIRIT SUSTAINED?
## (*Some very personal thoughts on the spirit of cricket, then and now*)

"No, boys, you just don't do that!" The teacher in charge quickly called the small schoolboys, excitedly playing their first ever organised game, to order. A tiny batter, dashing for a run, had bumped into a slightly bigger fielder in mid-pitch and gone sprawling. There were excited yells of "Stump him!" (we didn't understand the difference between stumped and run out at that tender age) and a rush to get the ball to the nearest stumps until the teacher stopped it. Silence followed his intervention, and then one boy, greatly daring, asked "Why not, sir?" The teacher's answer was firm if difficult for us small boys to comprehend: "You just don't. We don't play cricket that way."

When I got home, my father told me that this particular type of accepted cricket conduct had just been highlighted at the dizzying Olympian heights of international cricket, as the teacher had probably been well aware. Dad related the incident among the demigods (which was how I regarded Test players at that impressionable age, though I didn't know the word yet.) The SA captain, Jackie McGlew, had collided in mid-pitch with an England fast bowler named Moss, while the throw-in from an England fielder had hit the stumps. The umpires had insisted that McGlew was out, though the England captain, Cowdrey, had tried to recall him. "But why did Cowdrey want to recall Jackie,

Dad?" I asked. My father explained in terms as firm but as difficult for a little boy to grasp as the teacher's earlier in the day: that was just the way cricket was played.

That was probably my introduction to the concepts of sportsmanship and 'spirit of cricket'. I gradually learned that cricket stood as a kind of parable for life in this respect; the Victorian phrase "It isn't cricket" was still occasionally used for unsporting behaviour in general. By the time I read about the Body-line series some years later, I understood the full devastating impact of the Australian captain's reported comment to the England manager: "Only one team out there is playing cricket." As I got to know the game's Laws, I gathered that the umpires in the McGlew-Moss-Cowdrey episode had been totally out of line in giving the batter out when the fielding side hadn't appealed and had no wish to do so. (The umpires often acted controversially during this unhappy 1960 series, sometimes dubbed 'The Worst Series Ever', especially in no-balling the SA quick Geoff Griffin for throwing – said to be part of an MCC campaign to eliminate all suspect actions after their team had been 'thrown out' of the last Ashes series).

On the specific scenario of sparing a batter who collides with a fielder, I have read of a Test match in which a famous Australian keeper, Wally Grout, passed the ball in his gloves over the bails without disturbing them, to a tacit nod of approval from his teammates and all onlookers. In more recent years, a SA ODI team broke the wicket in similar circumstances as a kind of formality, but nobody appealed. The maligned Hansie Cronje, who was captain, walked over to the umpires and made it clear there was no appeal. This was further evidence, if any were needed, of how wrong those 1960 umpires had been to send McGlew packing.

One such incident at international level happened in 2022., South Africa were playing a T20I in India when the home captain, Rishabh Pant, tried to sneak a single, ran into the bowler Rabada and was stranded. A young SA international debutant fielding at mid-on, Tristan Stubbs, secured the ball and merely had to toss it to a colleague waiting at the stumps. *Stubbs instead lobbed the ball over his teammate's head.* It wasn't the clumsy act of a nervous rookie, as some thought. From the replays I was certain Stubbs did it deliberately, a notable instant decision by a newcomer to do the sporting thing, acting no doubt on a deeply ingrained cricket ethic, even when it meant his side forfeiting the wicket of such an influential opponent. Had the stumps been broken, whether to appeal would have been a decision for SA captain Temba Bavuma, not the newbie Stubbs. The latter's chivalrous act made me think of his namesake Sir Tristan, one of King Arthur's knights, who saved the fair Iseult from an unhappy marriage (and in the process bowled the maiden over, so to speak).

On-field application of the spirit of cricket is an enormous and often controversial topic, as the Cummings-Bairstow stumping during the 2023 Ashes showed. I will mention only the biggest debate of the past and the one still very much raging. Body-line, to put it very briefly, was wrong, although it did make for compelling drama, as seen in **Bite 48**.

There has been increasing discussion in the early 2020s around several dismissals of the type which some still call 'mankading' – a very unfair slur on the memory of the fine Indian all-rounder Vinoo Mankad. The relevant Laws were tweaked in 2021 to make it clear that any bad sportsmanship lies with the non-striker stealing ground, not the bowler dismissing him (contrary to the common perception). Nevertheless, bowlers don't like doing it. A careful watcher of the game will notice that bowlers at the highest levels almost invariably give transgressing non-strikers at least one warning, and often several, before acting. Unless and until there is a radical change of the Law (one popular suggestion is to scrap the possibility of a run-out and instead penalise the batting side one run or more), I believe that the players' instinct and usual policy should be recognised as the fair solution to this moral dilemma.

    The players themselves in general like to play 'hard but fair' and conform to some norms that may seem outmoded in certain quarters and in other sports. I remember Vernon Philander saying in an interview just after he retired, referring to everyone he had ever played with or against, "We're all gentlemen." The spirit of cricket is an integral, valued and enduring part of the game. It has been drilled into long generations of countless cricketers of all sorts until it has become instinctive in most of them. Tristan Stubbs's spontaneous act during that T20I had its roots very deep in the game's DNA.

# H. PICKS AND PERSPECTIVES

*(Highlights and a lowlight of my own cricket-watching 'career', which segue smoothly into my choices of the best matches that follow)*

## 29. PERSONAL FANDOM
### *(Frazzling finishes I've experienced, or not experienced)*

We all remember where we watched those nerve-frazzling down-to-the-wire finishes, whether on our own TV at home, at a friend's house, in a sports bar, in a department store with TV sets, furtively at work (unless the boss is also a fan and lenient) or if we were very lucky, at the ground. That's provided we caught the final fingernail-biting drama in real time – hearing the result after the event and watching endlessly repeated highlights can never be the same. My own experiences have ranged from what I call a cricket watcher's coup, to a complete wipe-out caused by misjudgement of a game's prospects. I'll relate them in reverse chronological order again. You will recall the first three matches at least; all three have often been claimed as the Greatest, or GOAT, ODI.

**Lord's 2019 – The Scorched Remote:** England and New Zealand, both striving for their first World Cup title, were locked neck-and-neck to the very end, Super Over and all, and even then could only be separated by the artificial boundary countback. The trouble was, if you had any feeling for unsurpassed drama and pinnacles of excellence in any other sport but cricket, that Roger Federer and Novak Djokovic were fighting out what was probably the greatest ever Wimbledon final at exactly the same time. "Sod the tennis", wrote one Cricinfo editor afterwards; he was referring to a family disagreement over which spectacle to watch, of a kind that must have played itself out in countless one-television households around the world.

Mine was one; my wife and daughter are huge tennis fans and huge Federer fans (as was I under most circumstances, for many reasons beside that his mother is South African). Somehow we managed to catch both the practically simultaneous dual climaxes, Buttler running out Guptill and Djokovic clinching the final tie-breaker, as well as most of the preceding twin dramas. Oh for a split screen facility! The highly contested TV remote was hot to the touch by the time both epic finishes were done. For the multi-sports lover, it wasn't an occasion to say Sod either sport; it was merely Sod's Law at its most fiendish, frustrating the sports connoisseur.

**Wanderers 2006 – Giving up too soon:** "Australia 434/4". The visitors' final score after their innings was scrawled in chalk on a blackboard somewhere in the Cape Peninsula. I was on a bicycle taking part in what was then called the Argus Cycle Tour; I'd opted to do that rather than to watch the decider of the 5-match ODI series at the Wanderers. The en-route update left me with so little hope that SA could chase such a score, 8.68 RPO over 50 overs, that I decided to spend the sunny afternoon not in a sports bar but sampling some of Cape Town's infinite outdoor attractions.

The rest, as you know, is history. I could hardly believe my ears in the early evening when I heard what had happened. It was some days before I saw even saw a recording of the crucial ball of the match, not Boucher's winning hit in the 50$^{th}$ over but the ball before, when last man Ntini squeezed a match-tying single to third man; as his partner Boucher commented later, "I told Makhaya we couldn't lose by one run now!"

The home side's final run tally has become enshrined as shorthand for the match: 'the 438 game'. The New Wanderers Stadium for years had a signboard outside boasting of being the "Site of the Greatest Ever ODI". I left Johannesburg some time ago, but it may have been removed after the 2019 World Cup final. The claim is up for debate, as will be seen in the next Bite. As for me as a non-spectator that day, I do still regret giving up too early on SA's run chase. But not too bitterly; bat-dominant runfests, of which this was the ultimate one in ODI's so far, have never thrilled me overmuch.

**Edgbaston 1999 – Expensive Eyewitness View:** The moment is seared in the memory of every SA fan who watched it. The hard-fought World Cup semi-final against arch-rival Australia was there for the taking: the scores level, one run required off four balls, then three. Then Klusener and Donald somehow, never quite explained by either player, contrived to 'run each other out' – not literally of course, Donald was the man out; but it seemed and was often described that way in the endless post mortems. Saffer fans were screaming at their TV sets; I wasn't, because I was actually sitting in the crowd at Edgbaston.

I was visiting England mainly to watch the 1999 World Cup, unfavourable Rand-to- Pound exchange rate and all, and naturally was at this game. I'd noted that Australia had the better Net Run Rate, but had never expected the scores would be tied and this would be the tie-breaker – yet it had happened, and canary-clad Australians were embracing each other on the pitch as a distraught Donald and expressionless Klusener headed for the pavilion with as little communication between them as they'd had before the fatal non-run.

The two-hour train trip from Birmingham back to London consisted of exchanging banter with more canary-clad fellows, triumphant Aussie fans in their team shirts (no other Saffers in sight). The initial numbing patriotic disappointment soon gave way to a more objective appreciation of the classic cricket match I'd watched: a perfect balance between bat and ball and between two highly skilled sides right up to the pulsating end. Ever since 2006, I have defended the claims of this game to be the Greatest ODI against many who'd watched the 434/438 pretender at the Wanderers.

**Sydney 1994 – Luck of the Shift:** Two in the morning in the South African midsummer: the coolest time of what would be a scorching day. It was still two hours until my shift at the Radio News desk where I worked would begin. Far away in Sydney, the home side were chasing only 117 to win after the peerless (and now much missed) Shane Warne had mesmerised the SA batters, facing him for only the second time, to the tune of 12/128. Australia were about to resume on 63/4. As I had to rise early anyway, the chance of a thrilling finish was more than enough to bring me to work early. I put one of the array of TV sets onto the cricket.

As I arrived at the News desk, the overnight 63/4 became 63/5. In what became known as 'Fanie's Finest Hour', the SA pace/seamer Fanie de Villiers tore into the home batters for the entire morning, as Donald and then Brian McMillan shored up the other end. At 75/8 the match seemed South Africa's; but a $9^{th}$-wicket stand swung the pendulum back and the score past 100 in this game of tiny margins. Ten minutes before lunch in Sydney, there was a feeling of 'now or never' (later exactly confirmed by the SA players): if the innings and the match went to lunch, the last of the bowlers' fierce momentum would be gone and the home batters would canter to victory – and incidentally, after those same ten minutes I would have to begin my duties in

Johannesburg.

The rest, again, was history: Martyn drove carelessly to cover (losing his place in the unforgiving Australian Test setup for some years as punishment); and eight balls later, Fanie stood victoriously straddling the pitch like the Colossus of Rhodes (except that Jonty Rhodes, another colossus of the match, was rushing from backward point to hug Fanie), as a then young Glenn McGrath tried to bury his bat ostrich-like into the pitch after prodding back a caught-and-bowled.

Back in Johannesburg, I led with the sports story on early news bulletins with no objection from more senior editors: this was just months before South Africa's tense, fear-ridden political transition of April 1994, and any kind of nation-unifying morale booster was much needed. Afterwards and back with cricket, I came across very few other fans who'd got up early enough to catch all the drama. That is why I still call this particular two hours of spectatorship my *'cricket-watcher's coup'*.

## 30. SO WHICH WAS THE GREATEST ODI?
*(Here's my choice, what's yours?)*

This debate has been touched on several times in the foregoing Bite, so I may as well give my opinion now.

After the 2019 World Cup final, there seemed to be an almost kneejerk reaction that this match had claimed the mantle from any previous game. This seemed to be based largely on the context: it was the final of what is still seen as cricket's biggest tournament, and it went down to the last possible ball, not once but twice, in both regulation play and the Super Over. But I'd like to point out a few remarkable parallels with the match that I (among others) believe still holds the title of GOAT among ODI's, that 1999 Edgbaston WC semi-final.

\*Both matches were actually ties in terms of runs, settled only by means that many considered unsatisfactory.

\*Both ended with a desperate run-out.

\*Both saw a very difficult but potential boundary catch going for six very near the end when a dismissal could have settled the match. At Lord's, had Trent Boult caught Ben Stokes instead of palming the ball over the rope, it would have been England on the ropes with 21 required off eight balls and only the lower order left to get them. At Edgbaston, Australia's Tom Moody similarly missed Shaun Pollock and conceded the maximum just when SA were slipping behind the required run rate (but there is a big caveat in the alternative scenario here: Klusener being Klusener and in the form he was during that World Cup, he might just have smashed a required 15 or so off the last over without any reference to Donald!)

*Both had slightly jarring notes for the absolute cricket purist. In 2019, Stokes' 'six along the ground', with four coming from 'overthrows' off the back of his bat, seemed wrong to many who thought the umpires should have called dead ball (no reflection on the sportsmanship of Stokes, who clearly wanted to "give the runs back"). In 1999, the climax just seemed wrong to the purist, because such a clumsy botch-up at the end simply had no place in the intense, high-quality, near-flawless contest that had raged for the past 99 overs.

*Both matches featured opposing innings within the 200-250 range which, for many of us, makes for the best 50-over games: if the pitch and conditions are such that skilled batters have to work hard to keep up a rate of 4-5 RPO against skilled bowlers, you have the perfect balance between bat and ball. All this is only my opinion, but I believe that many share it.

For objective cricket reasons rather than the SA participation and my in-house view, I hold that Edgbaston 1999 still holds the palm. Among the cricket aficionados on an online forum Talking Cricket, some agree, while many choose a range of other games as the GOAT ODI.

# 31. AND THE GREATEST TEST?
## (*Too debatable for long discussion*)

Picking the Greatest Test match is a far more difficult task than its ODI counterpart. What criteria do you use? Players and play of the highest quality? Hard to determine, even with the painstaking analysis that the gifted super-statistician Anantha Naranayan, often featured on Cricinfo, has put into this question. Ebb and flow? Certainly a strong factor, whether the match was close throughout or swung dramatically during its course. A tense final day and finish? Almost indispensable. A close result? A strong factor, though not quite as indispensable. In the end the choice will be subjective. I'm going to wriggle out of making one choice and instead offer five. Two are drawn from all the Tests I personally have followed and three from all the earlier ones that I have read about – as described in vivid accounts by gifted authors. None involve South Africa, as I save those for a later section.

My two own-lifetime choices are both part of the game's more recent folklore and need no lengthy description, though the second one deserves a long aside. Both involved rare reverses (and ultimately series losses) for the powerful Australian team around the turn of the millennium. However, this wasn't a conscious criterion, except in that seeing the underdog win perhaps adds to the overall retrospective appeal of a Test (though in neither case was the underdog rated much below the Australians, so one can't talk of David and Goliath.)

The first is England's two-run win at **Edgbaston in 2005**, the third closest Test match ever in run terms. The drama and tension as Lee and Kasprowicz closed in on the target absorbed the entire cricket world, not just England and Australia. The fact that Australia would have taken a 2-0 series lead if they'd made it, giving them one hand on the Ashes urn, only added to the drama. And who will forget the picture of Flintoff consoling a tearful Lee at the end as an iconic image of sportsmanship at the moment of triumph and disaster?

The other is India's victory at **Eden Gardens in 2001**. India's fightback in their follow-on, like Edgbaston 2005, gripped the attention of the entire cricket world. The Laxman-Dravid stand must count as one of the greatest partnerships, no matter what criteria you apply.

(Now for the long aside. It's a curiosity that Australia, the most successful Test country, was the loser in each of the first three Test matches, spanning three centuries, won by a side that followed on. One was this Kolkata epic; one happened in an Ashes Test back in 1895; and the third was the 1981 Ashes 'Headingley Miracle' in which the senior Australian players Marsh and Lillee bet against their own side at the rank outsider odds being offered at one point. The Australian team's coach driver reportedly placed the bet for them and, following the mind-blowing reversal engineered by Botham and Willis, collected their winnings. Rob Steen, the author of *500-1: The Miracle of Headingley '81,* connects the whole episode to Lillee and Marsh's leadership of a faction in the Australian side set on undermining captain Kim Hughes (remembered in SA for leading two rebel tours a few years later). Steen wonders if, for the anti-Hughes brigade, "heads made promises that hearts were unable to keep." I believe, however, that Lillee and Marsh meant the bet as a prank and that today's Anti-Corruption Unit would probably have let them go with a reprimand.)

My choice of three Tests from before an earlier era is a tribute to both the matches themselves and the writers of the gripping accounts of them. The first —working backwards again – happened in **1963**, when I was born but not yet following Test cricket. Alan Ross captures all the tension of the **England-West Indies Lord's** classic in which, to quote him, "No advantage to either side (was) lasting throughout the match." What really kept the reader on the edge of his seat, almost like a spectator at the ground, was the final over: all four results possible up to (technically) the final ball, and Cowdrey coming in at the end with his arm in a cast, though as the non-striker (see also **Bite 43**).

Almost three years earlier (when I definitely wasn't following Test cricket) the Australian Test opener-turned-author Jack Fingleton actually called his account of the **1961 Australia-West Indies tie**, the first of only two in almost one hundred and fifty years of Tests, *The Greatest Test of All*. Here too the final over, with all four results possible and two dramatic run-outs, sounds as if it comes from a Boy's Own story and not a real-life event. The tireless Barbadian pacer Wes Hall thundered in to bowl the final over at both Lord's and the Gabba. Fingleton has him singing calypsos in the change-room long after the Gabba finish; I imagine Hall (later Sir Wesley) did the same even in the more decorous atmosphere of Lord's.

I include the **1930 Lord's Ashes Test** from before contemporary memory. It did have a lot going for it: the Indian prince K.S. Duleepsinhji made 173 in a day for England; a twenty one-year-old Bradman announced his genius to the world with a pulverising 254; the match sustained averages of 400 runs (outstanding even today) and 125 overs per day (unthinkable in today), while 29 wickets fell; and there was a finish within the four scheduled days, with just a hint that the match might turn on its head towards the end. All of this took place under perfect blue skies and sunshine throughout (in England!). The distinguished writer Neville Cardus, who wrote a memorable pen picture of the match (including the description of a Jonty Rhodes-style cheap dismissal of Bradman mentioned in **Bite 37**), called it "the match of every cricketer's desire." Cardus's word is good enough for me.

Finally, I have to break my rule of reverse chronology and mention two Tests that 'came out of left field' as I was wrapping up this book in December 2022 and then revising it for the last time in late 2023. Everybody enjoyed the surreal Pakistan-England First Test at Rawalpindi in late 2022. On the face of it, this Test qualifies: an exceptional first innings, 650+ in four sessions instead of the usual six that left time to coax a result out of a road of a pitch; and a tense finish with perhaps ten minutes of play left. And a similar argument could be made for the heart-stopping Wellington Test in February 2023, which rewrote two of the Test records mentioned above. When a Test ends with a result close to unique in *two* ways - one run separating the teams and one of them winning after following on it's hard *not* to call it one of the best ever. Both these Tests were direct products of England's new approach, discussed in **Bite 27** above. My only reservations are that Stokes' decision to enforce the follow-on in Wellington seemed simply misguided rather than bold; and a lingering hesitancy about the Benbaz style when taken to extremes - is white-ball-in-red-ball batting at 6.5 rpo necessarily better Test cricket? (See my comments in Bite 27, however.)

# I. SOUTH AFRICA'S INTERNATIONAL IMPACT

*(It seems to me there are two main ways in which South African cricket has impacted the world game in recent decades. One is SA's well documented under-performance in global limited overs tournaments, with nothing to show for years of trying, despite generally having the necessary talent available to win as often as most other countries do. How many World Cups or ICC Trophies have other teams won that the Proteas seemed to be capable of taking? I analyse their much-discussed under-performance here in novel terms. The other major impact has come by way of the large number of players born in South Africa who are now key parts of other national teams, a phenomenon that is barely noticed as a rule. I take a brief collective view of these players here.)*

## 32. SA AT WORLD CUPS: WHAT ALWAYS GOES WRONG? *(Dumb cricket? Dumb luck? Dumb mindset?*

"Someone could write a PhD in Sports Psychology on South Africa's performances at World Cups." The speaker was my nephew, but the idea must have been expressed countless times by Saffer fans. They've even giving up tearing their hair out every four years when the Proteas exit the 50-overs World Cup. Saffers by now have the same kind of frustrated resignation as English football fans. Some say that South Africa will win the CWC when England win the FIFA World Cup again (at least England achieved that once, albeit controversially, in 1966): it may just happen in our lifetimes, but don't hold your breath.

The two words used most commonly to sum up SA's perennial WC underperformance, 'jinx' and 'choke', have different connotations. 'Jinx' suggests bad luck; 'choke' suggests the players run into some kind of mental block when the stakes are high and chips are down. The latter, sometimes called in SA "the dreaded C word", is the most common explanation among Saffers, as my nephew's semi-tongue-in-cheek remark implied. But there have indisputably been cases of bad luck as well, enough to suggest there is a jinx at work. I believe there is a third subset: simply failing to play clever cricket when it counts. We could call this 'dumb cricket', using the word 'dumb' in its

American sense as also in Afrikaans *dom*. So in this Bite I'll call bad luck 'dumb luck', again in the American sense. And the mental block, the propensity to 'choke', can then be called 'dumb mindset'.

I will now use these three descriptions as shorthand for what went wrong at each World Cup since SA's debut in the tournament in 1992. You'll remember, or can read about, all of them; see if you agree with my diagnosis in each case.

**1992**: One of the most enduring off-field images in SA's collective sporting memory is that Sydney scoreboard reading in neon lights, "South Africa need 22 runs off 1 ball." The on-field requirement of 22 runs off 13 balls would have been a stiff task in those pre-T20 days, but McMillan and Richardson, strong batters both although not natural big hitters, were playing aggressively and would have had a good chance. In any case, conditions after the rain interruption were perfectly good for the match to be completed properly, and you had to wonder if the match officials shouldn't have exercised some discretion. The rain rules seem to have been unclear, as the officials vacillated: at one point they decided that South Africa needed 22 off 7, an unlikely but not impossible task. I'm not sure if anybody has ever worked out who would have won had the Duckworth-Lewis system been in force then. (It's been argued that SA were not that unlucky in the light of certain factors like Wessels' decision to bat with rain forecast; the fact remains that the rain came at the worst possible time for his side.)

A fairy-tale title for the fledgling New South Africa would not have been begrudged by anybody, except perhaps Imran Khan's Pakistan side and their nation. In any case, it seems fair to say this was a case of 'dumb luck' that ended SA's unexpectedly good run as debutants in the World Cup. As matters turned out, it would also have saved the Proteas and their fans three decades of CWC angst that still continues.

**1996:** South Africa exited their second World Cup at the quarter-final stage when they ran into a rampant Brian Lara after dropping Allan Donald. On a Karachi pitch requiring two spinners, the vastly experienced coach Bob Woolmer had to omit a quicker bowler, and chose to make it his pace spearhead. Lara's brilliant Nelsonian 111 set up an awkward target, on that pitch, of 265. Hudson and Cullinan were criticised by many for not scoring faster during their long key partnership. I didn't think at the time that they could have humanly done so without resorting to risks against the spin of Harper and Adams. When they finally did because they had to, both got out. Is it 'dumb luck' when one of the all-time geniuses of the game plays up to his best form against you? I don't think SA could have argued that, any more than England could have claimed to be unlucky whenever Bradman took a Test away from them. Lara making a big score was just part of cricket then. Was it 'dumb' to go in without Donald? Debatable: Donald might have got Lara early on, but probably not thereafter on that pitch. I don't believe South Africa could blame themselves or any of the three 'dumb' factors in this instance.

None of this stopped Saffer fans from being bitterly disappointed, especially as a World Cup victory would have completed a remarkable triple for the then two-year-old New South Africa after the rugby Springboks won the RWC at their first attempt and the national football team, the *Bafana Bafana* or 'Lads', took the African CAF title, likewise on their debut in the continental competition. An Afrikaans newspaper editor, consoling his readers not in the sport pages but in his main editorial, gave a colloquial translation of 'It's only a game' – "*Dis slegs 'n ou ghympie."* That kind of phlegmatic, wider-perspective acceptance of a sporting setback has never really gone down well in South Africa.

**1999**: It's tempting to just write 'enough said' about the Edgbaston classic. For many it's still the Greatest ODI, but most Saffers remember only that shambolic Klusener-Donald run-out. A side that needs one run off four balls with a set batter facing (a batter at the very top of his form) should be able to make that single somehow, *finished and klaar (*as the bilingual saying goes in South Africa*).* England's Sun newspaper, with its penchant for weak wordplay, had the unkind headline 'Klue-less!' next day; but the closest analysis of the fiasco will never be able to pin the blame specifically on either Klusener or Donald. It was simply a brain-freeze on the part of both.

Was this a 'choke' caused by the pressure of the occasion? Many fans said so and still do. For myself, I thought both highly experienced men failed to play 'smart', so my diagnosis here would be 'dumb cricket'. But the line between 'dumb cricket' and 'dumb mindset' is a thin one, and perhaps the two overlapped on this ever-infamous occasion.

**2003**: As the Durban rain became heavier, Mark Boucher slog-swept Muralidharan for six and raised his fist in triumph. In ghastly retrospect, it would have been better if he'd managed only a four and had had to seek another big hit off the next ball, the last one before the umpires took the players off. Instead, Boucher – mindful that if he got out at this point, it would put South Africa back on the wrong side of the Duckworth-Lewis equation – carefully dead-batted a fuller ball that he could quite easily have pushed for a quick single. Then Boucher ran for the pavilion with the other players. The scrap of paper in his pocket must have become sodden in the pelting rain, so the figure written on it probably became illegible as well as ill-omened. Boucher was not best pleased when he learnt the true match situation and outcome.

The South African camp had, of course, made the fundamental error (conveyed to Boucher by the 12$^{th}$ man on that scrap of paper) of assuming that the D/L par score was a figure that only had to be equalled and not surpassed by at least one run, as has been the case with targets for chasing sides since cricket began. As a result, the host side for this tournament tied with Sri Lanka instead of winning and failed to progress from their group. For the second World Cup in succession, South Africa went out with a tie rather than a defeat – but where Edgbaston 1999 had been a dramatic fiasco, Durban 2003 was a sorry farce.

The only consolation was that after this drastic 'learning curve', the Proteas would never make that particular mistake again. One wonders how many teams, after the introduction and clear explanation of the DLS, would have made the error in the first place. 'Dumb cricket' in this case was an understatement.

**2007**: That famous 438 ODI at the Wanderers a year earlier was, psychologically, a major underlying cause of this particular World Cup mess-up (to use a polite term). The Proteas had taken on the Australian attack in a record ODI chase and succeeded. For the group match against Australia in the World Cup just a few months later, on a Basseterre pitch known for runfests, critics were freely predicting that 400 would be a par score. In line with this mode of thinking, Australia's 377 was thought to be sub-par and SA looked to be on track to overhaul it. But Brad Hogg's left-arm wrist-spin (a type of attack that SA batters seldom played comfortably then, if ever) claimed key top-order wickets and SA fell short of 300. Captain Graeme Smith, still inspired by the 438 match, had been chanting the mantra of 'brave cricket' (a white-ball pre-echo of England's new approach to Test cricket in 2022?). One setback didn't seem any reason to abandon it, as the Proteas advanced to the semi-finals with their positive approach.

The problem was that not all pitches are as batter-friendly tracks as the Wanderers on a good day or Basseterre. The semi-final venue, Beausejour in St Lucia, played low and slow, and yet the Proteas mindset didn't change. Playing 'brave cricket', the SA top order charged down this different track to bowlers as brilliant as McGrath, as unrelentingly accurate as Bracken, and as fast as Tait. The result was predictable: South Africa lost quick wickets and could manage only 149, exiting another World Cup. It might have been different had they bothered to take a few of the 50 overs for 'sighters' of how the pitch was playing.

This over-aggressive approach was, for me, another case of 'dumb cricket', rather than 'brave'. At least this error was well intended and wasn't as basic as those made in 2003 and 1999. Australia at this time were very hard to beat, although not quite invincible. These factors prevent me from applying the title of the puerile Hollywood movie *Dumb, Dumber, Dumbest* to these three successive South African World Cup exits as a kind of hare-brained hat-trick.

**2011:** This was perhaps another outlier. South Africa had a quarter-final against New Zealand in Dhaka. The Black Caps were kept down to 221 and, even on a slow 'holding-up' pitch', the Proteas didn't anticipate too much trouble in overhauling it. That, perhaps, was the problem. I don't think they 'choked' under the pressure of the occasion; instead, I think they were a little complacent, not usually a fault associated with SA. Added to this was that the batting mainstay, AB de Villiers, was unnecessarily run out, which threw the whole simple-looking chase into disarray. Faf du Plessis, suddenly left with only the tail for company, did his best, but the match was past saving.

You could have called this complacency a kind of 'dumb mindset' and the run-out of AB 'dumb cricket', but for me these missteps were different in nature from those in the other World Cups. For me this exit was the most like 1996: just something that happens in cricket. In any case, this was one World Cup that I don't think SA could ever have won, suppose they had cleared the Kiwi hurdle. India, the senior of the three co-hosts with a fanatical nation behind them, and Australia, unbeaten since 1999 in any World Cup match, somehow seemed predestined to contest the final.

**2015:** The Auckland semi-final was a wonderful match, one of the best ODI's ever (South Africa seem to have been involved in many of these). But in my opinion, SA threw away this match with their worst case of 'dumb mindset' to date. In believing this I have to extend the most profound and respectful apologies to the Proteas captain on the day, A.B. de Villiers, who said categorically once he'd composed himself, "We didn't choke." If 'choke' means making unnecessary mistakes because the magnitude of the occasion has got to you mentally, I think this is exactly what SA did. Allow me a few analytical paragraphs on a gripping but flawed game to explain this view.

Have a look at the rest of the match after the exact halfway point of the Black Caps' innings (the $22^{nd}$ over of 43 allowed). That was when Ross Taylor, New Zealand's last senior batter, fell, leaving the home side at 149/4, halfway also to their target but tilting the balance towards South Africa. Then suddenly, during the decisive Elliott-Anderson stand that followed, the wheels came off for the fielding side. Catches were dropped or missed, by keeper Quinton de Kock among others, run-outs were fumbled, most notably by de Villiers himself at the bowler's end when Anderson had already given up. I heard someone comment despairingly at the venue where I was watching that the Proteas would have to get the next wicket bowled or LBW, as they seemed to have lost the ability to hold a catch. The comedy of errors continued right up to the last ball of the penultimate over. When Elliott put up the inevitable catch, three fielders circled under it, and none could hold on. Even the level-headed Kiwis forgot to run in the frenzy, leaving Vettori to face Steyn at the start of the last over, an error by NZ for once. But Vettori managed to get Elliott on strike to finish the business, whereas it was doubtful that a new batter (Henry) could have hit a six with Steyn only slightly missing his length.

If this extended run of schoolboy mistakes wasn't 'choking' under the pressure of the occasion, what was it? There was certainly some 'dumb luck' earlier in the match towards the end of the SA innings. De Villiers and Miller – as potentially destructive a partnership as you could find at this or any tournament – were in full cry and threatening to take their side's total beyond 400, when rain caused an interruption. When they came back, their rhythm had been broken: the two hit some powerful blows in the curtailed remaining overs, but also swung and missed a few times. The final revised target set for the Black Caps proved to be just gettable, whereas 400+ off the full 50 overs would have been a tall order even for their abilities.

Then there was the matter of an injured Philander replacing the in-form Abbott in the attack and not being as effective as the latter could have been, especially in the opening overs of the NZ innings when Brendon McCullum tore into Philander and set a foundation for the chase. The reasons for this change in the Proteas side were political and have been discussed far too often to need repetition. Call this an excuse if you like. In my schema, none of the three categories apply here. I don't think you can use 'dumb luck' to refer to something as fundamental and existential to South Africa as its post-apartheid political system; without the political transformation, South Africa would probably still not be taking part in World Cups or any other international matches.

But both the above factors, the bad luck of the rain interruption and the Philander excuse, would not have kept South Africa from winning had it not been for that appalling run of fielding errors. They seemed to be caused by some sort of mental buckling under pressure: 'choking' if you like. That is why, in the end, I think 2015 was mainly a case of 'dumb mindset'.

**2019:** This was the only 50-over World Cup so far, I believe, in which the South African squad of the time simply weren't good enough to win. Without the services of AB de Villiers, they were plain outplayed in the first three matches (predictably by England and India, less so by Bangladesh) and had no chance of advancing after that. The final real hope was snuffed out in yet another defeat by New Zealand, for the third World Cup in a row. This raised a worrying spectre of a 'bogey team' for the Proteas, if you buy into the theory that they carry psychological baggage from one tournament to the next. Perversely, after the Proteas had been eliminated, they beat Australia, then a strong contender for the title (affecting the semi-finals and possibly the whole outcome of the tournament).

Most Saffer fans saw this less as a con solation victory than yet another example of the team's mindset problems, performing well only once the result was of no account for them. (It was at this point that my nephew made the remark about the Proteas' World Cup record being a potential subject for a Sports Psychology PhD.)

(I've passed over T20 World Cups up to now, because South Africa has generally not been as much of a pre-tournament favourite in this format. However, it's impossible to ignore the Proteas' exit from the 2022 T20 WC, described as SA's worst 'choke' ever by most commentators – including Tom Moody, who played in the 1999 Edgbaston match. Granting all due credit to a fast-improving Dutch outfit, it was hard to imagine that SA would not have made as short work of them without the, perennially destructive, 'must-win game' pressure. And it was in a T20 World Cup that a senior Proteas team did reach a WC final at long last – see Bite 26.)

**Looking immediately forward:** CWC 2023 is approaching the end of the league stage as I check the proofs of this book for the very last time and make the very final revisions. SA's Proteas have, believe it or not, apparently come up with yet another form of 'choking': under-performance when chasing, or batting second that stands in stark contrast to their dominant performances when batting first. The contrast is a chasm: batting first, scores of over 300 securing wins of over 100 runs on each occasion; batting second, a defeat to World Cup rookies the Netherlands (see also last paragraph), a stuttering, nervy one-wicket win over Pakistan that should have been fairly straightforward, and a 243-run shellacking by an Indian side admittedly at the top of their game on their home turf, especially in bowling – but are they really *that* much better than SA? In terms of my analysis, it's hard to see this anything else than a variation on 'dumb mindset'. At least SA have finally laid the possible New Zealand bogey mentioned above by beating the Kiwis at a WC for the first time since 1999 – although it wasn't a must-win game, and as I write, there remains a tantalising possibility of a second SA-NZ clash, which would have to be the final. But barring what would now be a significant upset, there seems little chance that SA (or any other team, even Australia) can stop the all-conquering Indians from marching to their second World Cup triumph at home and third overall.

If the Proteas fall short again, Saffer fans, despite all the disappointments and hair-tearing frustration over three decades, will continue to renew their faith and optimism when each new 50-over World Cup rolls round. Again, they can take solace from the far longer vigil of the legions of English football fans at every FIFA World Cup from 1966 – sixty years or 15 tournaments before their next chance to break the drought in 2026. Hope springs eternal, or at least quadriennial.

# 33. SOUTH AFRICAN DIASPORA
## (*The ones that got away*)

There is a recent joke still heard – not entirely appreciated by England supporters – about the Irishman, the New Zealander, the two South Africans, the two Pakistanis, the West Indian and the four Englishmen who won the ICC World Cup in 2019. There is an older joke that takes the form of a riddle: "Where do the England team stay when they tour South Africa? With their parents." This one is obviously an exaggeration; but it is true that for about a twenty-year period from the mid-1980s to the mid-2000s, it was rare for an England team to play a series without at least one South African-born player in their ranks. Without detailed analysis of the players concerned, you could say the period lasted more or less from Allan Lamb and Chris and Robin Smith through to Kevin Pietersen, Andrew Strauss, Jonathan Trott and Matt Prior – and continues with the likes of Jason Roy, Dawid Malan, and very sporadically, Keeton Jennings and Brydon Carse.

(There had been a foretaste in the 1970s when Basil D'Oliveira and Tony Greig played together for England, sharing some significant partnerships. There was enormous irony in this alliance, not so much because of their vastly different backgrounds in their shared homeland, as because the two men – for very different reasons – were at the respective centres of two very different controversies bookending the decade and both fundamentally affecting world cricket.)

The South African exodus has of course extended to the two remaining SENA countries, to use cricket's acronym for South Africa, England, New Zealand and Australia. Marnus Labuschagne was preceded as a SA-born Australian international by Kepler Wessels. Wessels had the unique distinction (if that is the word) of playing *for a 'full house' of both the SA official and unofficial teams and both the Australian official and rebel teams.* (The timing of his career before, during and after SA's rebel era, meant that no sanction was ever applied against him. Far from being tagged 'mercenary' or anything like that, he was rewarded with the captaincy of SA in its epoch-making World Cup debut and return to Test cricket, once Clive Rice and Jimmy Cook were deemed to be too old for the post. In fairness, Wessels could not be criticised for any of this; he was just fortunate enough to be in the right place at the right time, every time.)

New Zealand has at times threatened to replace England in the above joke about where touring teams stay in South Africa (with a similar degree of jocular exaggeration). Their SA-born players of the fairly recent past have included two of their Test keeper-batters, B.J. Watling and the diminutive Kruger van Wyk. They still have the short-ball specialist in their formidable pace attack, Neil Wagner. Glen Phillips is capable of exercising a devastating influence in any T20 game, and could well translate this ability to longer formats. (Willem Ludick has played only at domestic level, for Central Districts, but deserves a mention as one of only two bowlers to have conceded 43 runs off a single over in an A-list match.)

The prime 'Saffekiwi' example, though, is of course Devon Conway, and I can reveal a strangely clear memory in his regard.

I recall a local reporter writing of Conway at U-19 level that he would be "the next Barry Richards". Conway failed to live up to that exalted prediction over a decade in South Africa, but suddenly blossomed after emigrating, KP-like. Unlike Richards, Conway is left-handed and only occasionally shows flashes of the BAR grace, for example with his flowing cover drive. However, his double century on Test debut, a rare achievement, gave promise of Richards-like output. This would not be sustained, but Conway has excelled as an all-format opener, proving highly effective in ODI's and T20's – as Richards no doubt would have done had he played in the shorter formats. Conway is not quite a Richards; but I still wish I could remember the name of that perceptive SA scribe, whose startling assessment of a young player has been at least partially vindicated.

SA expats can be found in other international teams too. Curtis Campher plays for Ireland; Brad Wheal for Scotland; 'Rusty' Theron for the USA (no relation of his Hollywood namesake Charlize). A number of SA-born-and-raised players have appeared for the Netherlands, including the formidable batter Ryan ten Doeschate. Four of them helped their ancestral country to eject their compatriots from the 2022 T20 World Cup in what was perceived as a sensational upset (unless, of course, you put it down to SA's apparently incurable 'choking' complex at global tournaments, discussed in the last Bite.)

And does any of this signify anything; am I trying to make any point? Not really. It has to be admitted that South Africans have always seemed to take an undue degree of vicarious pride in the performances of these players – even those who emigrated with their parents as children, leaving SA with little real claim on them. Countless times in sports pubs and clubs, viewing the cricket on a high-mounted TV screen as one of these players excels in the service of his adopted country, I've heard comments along the lines of "He's from South Africa – what do you expect?" or occasionally, "Imagine if he were playing for us." SA fans also enjoy picking an XI of expatriate Saffers playing for or in other countries. The top three in the order would be as strong as or stronger than most Test sides, whichever way round you choose to put Conway, Malan and Labuschagne (with Roy possibly in there for a white-ball match).

None of this is taken seriously, of course. An expat coming in to bat against South Africa will face a little banter, often in Afrikaans or even Zulu, from the fielders stationed close to the wicket, as well as a few choice remarks from the spectators if the game is in his native country. It's all good-natured and there is no grudge or animosity involved. There is no need to elaborate on the changing political, social and financial conditions in South Africa that caused these players, or their parents, to relocate. Migration under various pressures, including vast population movements of all races, is deeply embedded in the nation's history and collective consciousness. No South African is ever going to criticise another one for taking his chances and extending that trend.

# J. SOUTH AFRICA: INSIDER VIEWS

*(Non-South African readers can skip this entire section, but I suggest you don't. As an outsider, you may want to hear my impressions – many from personal experience – of how cricket fared under the former enforced racial segregation in South Africa, intensified in the mid-twentieth century under the name apartheid. I was fortunate enough to be born on the advantaged side of the racial divide, but always looked out for glimpses of hope in the cricket endeavours of those on the other side. On the technical side, you may wonder why South Africa has produced so few top-flight wrist spinners, with either hand, since a brief flowering of leg-spinners over a century ago. I also look at the pick of South African international players; at SA cricket families that have excelled over two generations or more; at major SA grounds, especially their less formal spectator areas; and choose my favourite South African matches. International connections and context are given in several of these Bites.)*

# 34. DIVISION TO UNITY
## *(In a tragically divided society)*

It took exactly a century for South African test teams to become representative. South Africa played its first Test in 1889. The United (effectively meaning racially united) Cricket Board of South Africa was formed in 1989. For the intervening hundred years, the team officially representing South Africa as recognised by the ICC, consisted wholly of white players under a white administration, playing only against England, Australia and New Zealand. Players of other races had their own structures and governing bodies, as noted below. I want to give not a history, but only a few personal insights and experiences of this division of South Africa's cricket, reflective of centuries of segregation in its society at large.

### a. A Community's Passion for Cricket

Hashim Amla is South Africa's only Test triple centurion and rates as one of its greatest batters ever. Keshav Maharaj is perhaps the country's best left-arm spinner for fifty years and possibly longer. He once took 11 of the first 12 Sri Lankan wickets to fall on a rank turner on the island, and in 2022 took two seven-fors in successive Tests against Bangladesh. The two players represent a culmination, a realisation, of the long-suppressed potential of a whole community.

South Africa's Indian-descended people have a deep passion for cricket, something for which I can cite personal observation. They used to pack out the enclosure at Durban's Kingsmead ground that was reserved for people classified as 'non-white' under apartheid laws. This was the case for Test matches as well as all the provincial games of the team then called Natal. They displayed more bubbling enthusiasm than any of the other spectators. This caused me to muse on how they must love the game.

Most of us need a partisan loyalty to really enjoy our sport: we need to 'root' for one team, to exult in its successes and groan at its setbacks. Not so the South Africans of Indian descent under apartheid. There was no reason why they should support all-white teams representing a country that denied them full citizenship. But generally they also didn't make a point of backing South Africa's Test opponents. No, I could tell these SA Indian fans were at Kingsmead because they loved cricket for cricket's sake and cheered good play when they saw it, never mind which side the batter, bowler or fielder was on. You don't get a purer passion for the game than that.

The community has displayed talent in multiple fields and was always going to produce cricketers of the highest quality. When they finally gained full access to the opportunities for success in top-level cricket, Amla and Maharaj, and many others at provincial level, showed what the community was capable of. These players weren't the first from the South African Indian community of such calibre, of course. A predecessor of Maharaj managed to beat apartheid, as I explain next. Many have succeeded at provincial level. Amla and Maharaj will not be the last to play and excel for South Africa.

**b. When Baboo beat apartheid**

Ismail 'Baboo' Ebrahim's great moment had a complicated context, which needs to be recalled. We have to go back to the time before South Africa's rebel tour era of 1982-90 (which today is remembered as little more than a footnote, an eight-year irritation to mainstream world cricket. Its most notable effects were the bans on England opening kingpin Graham Gooch for three years and Lawrence Rowe of the West Indies for life.)

What is almost forgotten today is a brief period before the rebel tours, when the SA authorities were still seeking a less aggressive back door into international cricket. Cricket patron D.H. or Derrick Robins sent three teams to South Africa in the 1970s that at least extended SA's strongest team and kept up the morale of Test-starved fans and players. When these tours dried up, South Africa's cricket governing bodies brought in a side called the International Wanderers in 1976. The series it played against a 'South African Invitation XI' was, in my opinion, more interesting than any of the rebel tours that followed.

I just said South Africa's cricket governing BODIES. The plural reflects the fact that cricket, like most things in apartheid, was divided along racial lines. The story of the multi-racial (in effect non-white) cricket bodies, their players and their competitions, has been comprehensively documented by historian Andre Odendaal and others. Apart from the odd multi-racial game in defiance of the apartheid authorities, these structures had little to do with the white-run, ICC-recognised establishment that had always chosen the country's Test teams from white players – but some of them relented briefly in the mid-1970s.

At that time, in the hope that helping SA gain readmission would lead to more inclusive national teams in the future, the multi-racial bodies made their players available for selection against the International Wanderers. Several of them were duly picked. Many or most white fans, lacking political insight and stuck in the mindset of the apartheid mantra "Keep politics out of sport", criticised these selections as mere tokenism – until they were all proved wrong by Baboo Ebrahim.

Ebrahim's Indian-descended community, as just noted, usually packed out their segregated enclosure at Kingsmead in Durban for any big match. As a boy, he was watching a Test match there when the England left-arm spinner Johnny Wardle suddenly used his wrist to spin down an off-break (a 'chinaman' as it was then known) that baffled the local hero, 'King of Kingsmead' Roy McLean, and bowled him through the gate. Such a delivery was virtually unknown in South Africa; and Ebrahim, himself a budding orthodox left-arm spinner, decided from that moment to add the ball to his armoury. By his own account the extra weapon helped him greatly in the 'alternative' competitions, where he had to play his cricket.

But that changed in 1976 when Ebrahim was chosen for the South African Invitation XI's third match against the International Wanderers, who were leading the series 1-0. Now at Kingsmead as a player, Ebrahim ran through the visiting team's second innings with figures of 6/66, not quite satanic but certainly a revelation to all the critics who thought a white left-arm spinner (respected names like Henwood, Kourie and de Vaal were around) should have played. Among his victims were two Ashes captains and leading batters, Greg Chappell and Mike Denness. (Whether Ebrahim here deployed the left-arm off-break he'd learnt from Wardle almost twenty years earlier, is not clear from accounts of the match). Ebrahim became overnight a candidate on his merits, race and politics aside, for any South African national or quasi-national team that might be selected.

But politics in the most violent form intervened a few months later. The bloody Soweto riots, a seminal event in the struggle against apartheid, shocked the world and led to a sudden and severe tightening of sports sanctions against South Africa. In cricket, relations between the different domestic governing bodies hardened, no more 'invitation' teams came, and the next international visitors would be the first team of proscribed rebels in 1982.

Baboo Ebrahim did break through into white-run 'establishment' cricket a few years later, being selected for Natal provincial teams. But the magic moment had passed. Ebrahim had, however, for one brief shining Camelot afternoon, showed South African cricket what it had missed and would miss until political change made the national team representative.

**c. Timol vs Lillee**

I have a personal memory along the same lines from watching one day of that International Wanderers match in Durban, which still carries a certain poignancy. Baboo Ebrahim wasn't the only SA Indian (for want of a better term) playing in that match and thought to be out of his depth. A batter named Farouk Timol, who also excelled in 'non-mainstream' cricket, played a less obvious part in the SA XI's win. He made only seven and six, duly recorded as his entire first-class batting figures by the official statistics in Cricinfo. But that HS innings – which I watched carefully – wasn't your ordinary seven-run knock: it was significant in the match context and included sustained defiance of one of the best and most dangerous fast bowlers ever.

Timol resolutely partnered the great Graeme Pollock in a half-century stand that was crucial in the low-scoring match. Timol's role was to hold his end up stoutly against world-class bowlers: the English left-arm spin pair of Underwood and Edmonds, and the fearsome Australian pace trio of Gilmour, Hurst and the legendary Dennis Lillee. Lillee in particular subjected Timol to a barrage of fiery short stuff, which he stood up to bravely. Four of Timol's seven runs came when Lillee sent down a much slower ball too full and outside off; Timol, pinned to the back foot for most of his innings, came smartly forward and cracked it through the covers.

Some fans sitting near me said condescendingly, liquor-fuelled and with more than a hint of racism, "Lillee must have felt sorry for him and given him a lolly. Lillee's lolly, hahaha!" I knew better; I spotted from the ring that Lillee, in the best tradition of Keith Miller and other predecessors, had tried to outwit the stubborn Timol with a googly by way of variation, but missed his length. And of course, I knew – especially after England's torrid Ashes series of 1974/5 – that Dennis Lillee never felt sorry for a batter in his life.

Nobody notices race in SA teams any more, which is as it should be, but Ebrahim and Timol were trailblazers for Amla, Maharaj and no doubt many more players of the highest order still to come.

#### d. The other once excluded communities

I won't dwell at the same length on South Africa's other two communities that were once excluded from the cricket and every other mainstream. (There's no real reason for this other than that I was based in the Durban area as a student and watched many matches at Kingsmead, including that memorable International Wanderers game.) For non-SA readers, one of these is the country's majority of black Africans, and the other is the mixed-race community known historically as Coloureds. Even putting names to these communities can be a political minefield. With apologies to anyone offended, I will use the terms blacks and 'Coloureds', the latter in quotes (the phrase 'so-called Coloureds' that some insist on is rather cumbersome).

The 'Coloured' community, thanks initially to its base in Cape Town where British influence began in the early 1800's, has played organised cricket for around two centuries. Andre Odendaal has described this in detail. I will add only that with this kind of background, there have probably been many 'Coloured' players who could have achieved the highest level with more opportunities. This was amply illustrated by 'Krom' Hendricks, widely acknowledged as the best bowler in South Africa in the 1890s, but excluded from national teams because of his race. Seven decades later, little had changed: Basil D'Oliveira had to emigrate to play top-class cricket and forced his way into the England team. (The turmoil caused by his selection to tour South Africa in 1968, bringing the cancellation of that MCC tour and hastening South Africa's ostracism after only one more incoming tour, is well documented. I will add only that D'Oliveira conducted himself with the utmost dignity throughout the affair, was not personally blamed by most SA fans even in those days, and is still justly honoured by the trophy for Test cricket's second oldest rivalry named after him.)

So it was no surprise that 'Coloured' players were selected for Proteas teams not long after SA's readmission, starting with the left-arm spinner Omar Henry, also known as a captain of Scotland. After "Mac"-Henry, Paul Adams, Ashwell Prince, J.P. Duminy and Vernon Philander were fixtures in the national side for years. Prince was a prolific batter and became South Africa's first 'non-white' captain (again, I use the term for want of a better one) on a tour of Sri Lanka in 2006. Philander was one of the more feared bowlers in world cricket when conditions were right. And as I write, South Africa has a 'new KP' in Keegan Petersen, but this one is staying firmly at home.

The black community, by contrast, had very limited

exposure to cricket before well into the twentieth century, and limited interest; football (or soccer as it's generally called in SA) was their consuming sports interest. Nevertheless black cricket was able to throw up Frank Roro, whose domination was such that he compared, in context, with W.G. Grace, Donald Bradman or George Headley. One would love to have seen Roro batting for a representative SA Test team with contemporaries like Nourse, Mitchell or Rowan. The Eastern Cape (Eastern Province and Border in cricket terms), where British-backed mission stations propagated cricket from the nineteenth century, has long been a haven of black cricket. It was no surprise when the area produced the pioneering Makhaya Ntini, as well as Mfuneko Ngam, who could have made as much impact as Ntini, had his career not been cut short by injuries. With today's far greater – though still far from complete – equality of opportunity, Kagiso Rabada, Lungi Ngidi, Temba Bavuma and Ayabonga Khaka are just some of the standard bearers.

**e. The situation today**

Happily, hardly anyone notices the race of a South African player in the 2020s. It's almost a non-issue already, except for those trying to make it an issue. (The recent past, the subject of a controversial CSA investigation that brought unsuccessful racism charges against Graeme Smith and Mark Boucher, is another matter; my concern is with the present and future.) The racial 'quota' prescribed by CSA but not strictly observed, is becoming almost superfluous.

The heartening reality is that by a process of natural evolution, the national team, selected almost completely on merit, has become multi-racial without artificial compulsion. That is how it should be in the Rainbow Nation of Nelson Mandela (a product of that Eastern Cape mission school background, who mentions his love for cricket in his autobiography *Long Walk to Freedom*). The integration and reconciliation process envisaged by Mandela is far from complete, in cricket as in much of South African society. But in cricket, at least it is well advanced.

# 35. THE CURIOUS RISE AND DISAPPEARANCE OF SOUTH AFRICAN LEG-SPIN… (*With reflections about leg-spin in other countries*)

Four in one team; then a bare handful for a century and longer. A lofty spike on the graph is followed by a long flat line, like a series of maiden overs, that still continues. This sums up South Africa's strange story in the difficult art of leg-spin.

Four 'leggies' in a single XI sounds like the sort of team you might have picked for an Asian dustbowl pitch of years ago; but SA actually fielded such an attack in the early twentieth century – when their own pitches were laid with matting. They could do so without weakening the batting too much because one of the four leg-spinners, Aubrey Faulkner, was one of the great all-rounders of all time, probably the greatest one to bowl only spin. The other three had interesting names. Two were of German descent: Vogler (meaning Fowler, like a much later England opener, and appropriate for one who ensnared batters like birds) and Swartz, meaning black, an interesting counterpoint to the fourth member of the quartet, White. Part of their success was down to the fact that all four had mastered the recently invented googly. Swartz apparently even lost the orthodox leg-break: it is said that an England team received a cablegram saying "Swartz only turns from off" – an early case of mass communications affecting tactics.

After these four, the species suddenly goes almost extinct: South Africa have barely had another specialist leg-spinner of note ever since. The exception that proves the rule is Xenophon Balaskas, one of the heroes of SA's famous series-winning victory at Lord's in 1935; but his success was a one-off. After him we find only sporadic cases: names like Ian Smith (not the former Rhodesian leader) in the 1940s and Jackie du Preez (who was indeed Rhodesian), and none could hold down a regular place in the Test side.

Leg-spin was practically unknown on the field in South Africa when I was growing up in the 1960s and 70s, just a theoretical construct even for school and club coaches. I remember the buzz of interest at the first 'A-list' match I ever attended when an English leg-spinner, R.N.S. Hobbs, came on to bowl for the MCC in a minor tour match in Benoni. Few of the crowd had ever seen real leg-spin in action. It was disappointing. Hobbs (no relation of the legendary Sir Jack, which also disappointed a few spectators) gained little turn on the rock-hard Highveld pitch, though the local batters played him with a wariness born of complete unfamiliarity with his technique.

Despite the absence of leg-spin in SA, Afrikaans, which has developed its own cricket terminology, came up with a wonderful translation of 'googly'. *Goëlbal*, a 'guile-ball', carries the sense that such a delivery is like a spell cast by a bowler-sorcerer to bewitch the batter.

It was a cruel stroke of fortune that the only world-class leg-spinner the country has produced since World War I, Denys Hobson of Western Province, played exactly during the isolation period of the 1970s and 80s. Hobson's quality was at least recognised by Kerry Packer's circus, which selected him for their

World XIs in World Series Cricket.

Since isolation ended, it has been no different. SA's only leg-spinner of note has been an import from Pakistan, Imran Tahir, known for his excited dashes as far as cover or midwicket every time he took a wicket, or even further if it was a big one – but sadly these dashes never happened often enough in Test cricket. 'Immy' was one of the most effective bowlers in the world in either T20 or ODI games, but for some reason – possibly to do with batters being able to wait for the bad ball without worrying about run rate – never really came off in Tests. For a long time, SA batters collectively had a distinct chink in their armoury against good wrist spin due to lack of exposure to it; the likes of Miller and de Kock, thanks to extensive IPL play, were overcoming it by the 2020s.

Asian bowlers seem to have spin, including wrist spin, in their blood. And yet a country outside the sub-continent has produced a glittering, almost unbroken, chain of star leg-spinners, including the two best ever. Or perhaps the metaphor for Australian leggies should be a mountain range: major peaks like Mailey, Grimmett and Benaud; minor but still prominent peaks like Ring, Jenner, Holland or today's Zampa and Swepson; two mist-shrouded peaks in the 'mystery' folded-finger spinners Iverson and Gleeson (though neither would be regarded as 'mystery' bowlers today, in an era when the carom ball is standard even outside Asia); and towering above all – even over the subcontinent's eminences topped by Mt Kumble – the two ultimate summits in O'Reilly as K2 and Shane Warne as Everest.

Is all this mostly to do with a country's cricket 'culture'? Australia have as much of a leg-spin culture as the Asian countries; SA and England, these days, do not. The peerless Shane Warne is no longer around to spread his trade secrets (see

**Bite 23**), following in the footsteps of one of his predecessors, Arthur Mailey. Mailey, an artist of the painting type off the field, was once scolded for disclosing his bowling secrets to the English arch-foe. He retorted, "Bowling is an art; and as such, international."

South Africa needs to rediscover leg-spin in its cricket culture, with or without the help of a stellar exponent like Warne. No team will ever field four specialist leg-spinners again as SA did over a century ago. But even one home-grown specimen would be welcome in the Proteas attack.

## 36. ...AND THE STRANGE STORY OF SA LEFT-ARM WRIST SPIN
### (*With some thoughts on such bowling internationally, including finding a good name for it*)

The last Bite deliberately omitted any mention of the mirror image of leg-spinners: those bowlers who also use their wrists to impart spin, but are left-handed. This is because both the genre, and South Africa's experience of it, have some very distinctive features. For a start, left-arm wrist spin developed differently – and here there does seem to be a strong SA connection.

The name C.B. 'Charlie' Llewellyn is a controversial one in South African cricket history, as there is dispute whether he can be regarded as the first 'non-white' to play a Test for South Africa, almost a century before Omar Henry. The concern here is not with that debate, but with Llewellyn's bowling method. Reports from the 1890s suggest that he bowled left-arm finger spin, but often varied it with balls that broke from off. In the nature of spin bowling before the carom ball was invented, *Llewellyn probably achieved this with wrist spin.* Only recently has this South African been given credit for introducing this variation on left-arm orthodox spin.

Llewellyn apart, left-arm spinners are known to have turned

some balls from the off since at least the 1920s, but it was Ellis Achong, the Chinese-Trinidadian who played for the West Indies in 1933, who apparently gave the delivery its former name (though Neville Cardus traces the term 'chinaman' to the Yorkshire dressing room of the 1920s). I have never liked the story of how England's Walter Robins (or in one version, Patsy Hendren) was deceived by such a ball from Achong and grumbled, "Done by a bloody Chinaman!" For one thing, it may not be true: Robins was himself a very good right-handed leg-spinner, and could have been expected to pick the wrist-spun delivery. But more seriously, I was brought up in a liberal white household where the many derogatory racial terms then common in South Africa (but now illegal) were outlawed, and I always thought Robins' outburst and the term 'chinaman' smacked of similar racism. So I was glad when Wisden used its authority to proscribe the term in 2017 and Cricinfo followed suit in 2021. What, though, will replace it as a description?

The answer lies in the evolution of this type of bowling. It was inevitable after this variation proved successful that in due course, some left-arm slow bowlers would drop the finger spin altogether and become mainly or wholly wrist spinners. The first such bowler at Test level (Llewellyn apart) came just a few years after Achong, Australia's L.O.B. Fleetwood-Smith. His initials say it all – LOB, Left-arm Off-Break! (Fleetwood-Smith was a talented but troubled character who repays study; you would not be the first to note the Hitler lookalike moustache he sported during the Nazi dictator's heyday.)

What then can we call the 'left-hander's googly' – the 'wrong 'un' that Fleetwood-Smith and his successors, notably Brad Hogg, inevitably developed in mirror image of the right-handed googly, thus spinning away towards the slips? What else but LLB, Left-handed Leg-Break, borrowing the abbreviation for a legal degree? But this might be confused with the orthodox left-arm spinner's stock ball. Commentators and analysts may have as much trouble finding appropriate terms for all these varieties as some batters, especially South Africans, have in picking them.

Meanwhile, let's go back to the South African history of LWS, as Left-arm Wrist Spin is 'officially' abbreviated. Like leg-spin in the country, it has a long barren period, but unlike it, the species has reappeared. Exactly a century (less three months) after Charlie Llewellyn first bowled LWS for South Africa in a Test, Paul 'Gogga' Adams did so in December 1995. His unique action ("unorthodox" is an understatement – see **Bite 10**) could not conceal the basic mechanics: even though he gripped the ball with only his thumb and forefinger, adding to his uniqueness, the fact remained Adams used his wrist to generate turn in both directions and was therefore a genuine LWS. More recently, at the time of writing, Tabraiz Shamsi, a kind of new Adams, has become a successful white-ball bowler. Shamsi's stock LOB, when flighted, drifts teasingly away to off before breaking in (the way Fleetwood-Smith once reportedly bowled Hammond), unlike the sub-continental LWS's like Sandakan and Kuldeep Yadav, who tend to have a flatter, straighter flight.

It's heartening, amid the dearth of leg-spinners in SA, that Adams and now Shamsi – both from Cape Town, whatever that signifies – have come on the scene within the last thirty years. The two may help to instil a new inclination towards LWS, or wrist spin generally, among aspiring young spinners that, along with right-handed leg-spin, has been missing in South African cricket culture.

LWS's place in that culture follows a pattern across cricket countries similar to leg-spin, unsurprisingly. South Asia produces them regularly. Australia has about one a generation – think Hogg (who played top-level white-ball matches well into his 40s); Michael Bevan (primarily a batter, but effective when bowling in tandem with Warne, and see **Bite 14**); and earlier Lindsay Kline (who once took a hat-trick against SA, but is better remembered historically for his batting role to the last ball of the first Tied Test). West Indies had Achong. England have had hardly any in their long history; Johnny Wardle seems to have mixed up LWS with orthodox left-arm finger spin. He had a momentary but profound effect on the bowling of South Africa's 'Baboo' Ebrahim, as noted in **Bite 34**.

It remains to suggest a new vivid term for an LWS, which is just a descriptive acronym, now that 'chinaman' has gone its deserved way. It's not too late to give SA's Llewellyn belated recognition as the apparent inventor of the genre. The Australians long called a googly a 'bosie' after its English inventor, Bernard Bosanquet (who went on a North American tour with Llewellyn, but let's not get too complicated). So an LWS could deservedly be called a 'Charlie' or a 'Buck', another nickname given to Llewellyn. Buck rhymes, oddly, with Fleetwood-Smith's nickname, Chuck, so perhaps 'buck' for these bowlers' stock LOB and 'chuck' for their 'wrong 'un'. An LWS bowler turning it both ways could thus be a 'buck-and-chuck'. However, even Australians, despite Fleetwood-Smith's nickname, might draw the line at using the latter term for any legitimate delivery.

# 37. MY PICK OF SOUTH AFRICAN PLAYERS
## *(SA players etched in the memory)*

The problem here is really who to leave out. Only a limited number could be included in each discipline. I borrow the term 'The Magnificent Seven' from the classic Western with little apology, as it's been applied to Kruger National Park elephants and many others. But it's also convenient for SA international batters, as exactly seven stand out for me. Six of them I watched live and often: the magnificent Quartet that helped South Africa to do so well from around 2008 to 2014; plus two peerless batters just before isolation – and with them I place a legend from before my time that I read and heard much about. Seven will also do for the bowlers. I talk about only two fielders, for reasons that will be made clear. Again, I work backwards chronologically. These are personal memories and impressions (my own and occasionally others'), with little mention of figures and averages that are freely available.

### A. THE MAGNIFICENT SEVEN BATTERS

**A.B. de Villiers** was just 'Superman', with a hand-eye co-ordination that enabled him to do almost anything in sport (those who knew him as a schoolboy said he could have become a Springbok flyhalf or an international squash player, but thank goodness he chose cricket). It always surprised me that he didn't bowl seriously, though I'm sure he could have if he'd put his mind to it: he fielded superbly, but switched for a while to keeping wicket in Test matches, well up to the required standard, without a blink. In his batting, the same versatility was always present. His prolific scores in Tests were compiled with technical correctness, only occasionally improvising shots. But it was his 'Mr 360' ability in limited-over games that is legendary. This has been described too often for me to go into it, except to say that he would move with dazzling quickness to make room for a shot, then twirl his wrists to direct the ball to almost any desired corner of the field. The best recorded visual illustration – there are many – is probably the YouTube of his record 150 off under 50 balls against the West Indies: it was in one of those Wanderers ODI's where the Proteas dress in pink, and the worthy cause of fundraising for the battle against cancer could hardly have had better publicity.

In the last part of his career, AB pirouetted between availability and retirement in a way reminiscent of his pirouettes as a white-ball batter; I think the 2015 World Cup semi-final broke his heart. But his fierce dedication and extraordinary performances during his long years in Proteas outweighed any criticism of other phases. (I return to AB later with a light-hearted fantasy in which he matches his talents against an equally gifted man in another field.)

**Hashim Amla** looked so 'regal' and 'majestic' at the crease that I have to abandon my general policy of avoiding all racial or ethnic stereotyping and evoke his northern Indian ancestry. If this wasn't aristocratic, it should have been: had a Mogul emperor played cricket and possessed the talent, I think he would have batted like Amla. The nicknames given to him like 'The Mighty Hash' or 'Hashim the Magnificent' somehow reflected this comparison, however unconsciously on the part of the fans. His height allowed him to play like the classic tall batter, especially when he drove through the off-side field or used his wrists to find the square-leg or midwicket boundary. He could do all of this from either foot, but I liked his front-foot strokes on either side of the wicket best.

When Amla looked a little harassed in the rare T20I's he played, a fan tweeted that "you don't use your Rolls Royce for drag racing", the fan could have mentioned the Aston Martin of 50-over cricket, in which Amla was also prolific. But long formats, especially Tests, were his glory. Lucky Surrey to recruit a batter like Hashim Amla illuminating multi-day cricket for the final phase of an illustrious career.

**Jacques Kallis** made the textbook look beautiful (my rephrasing of Neville Cardus' description of England's classic opener R.H. Spooner, "he put a bloom on the orthodox"). Kallis seemed to play every shot exactly as shown in the MCC textbook and do it in the most graceful and eye-pleasing manner. I especially liked to see his forcing off-side stroke perfectly balanced on the back foot with his front foot up in the air: he made the shot look almost balletic, despite being far more broad-shouldered than any ballet dancer. Added to the lovely strokeplay was his exceptional power of concentration and focus: as opponents admitted, Kallis batted in a 'bubble' that they simply couldn't penetrate. The Australians looked for a chink in his technical armour, but couldn't find one; they tried psychology, sledging him to achieve 'mental disintegration' (Steve Waugh's phrase), but Kallis' bubble held firm. All of this was what underpinned his high number of Test centuries and other outstanding statistics. And he could bowl a bit too, as we'll see.

**Graeme Smith's** virtues as a batter always leaned towards the Pole B type - determination, resolution, application, courage – rather than Pole A – elegance, grace, style, flourish. I greatly respected his ability to accumulate runs once he was set, but have to admit that I never took the same pleasure in watching him bat as much as I did the rest of the Quartet. His strokes were meaty and powerful, but somehow looked more laboured than effortless. That closed-face quasi-drive he played from around the line of off-stump through mid-on or midwicket always looked like a risky 'drag' across the stumps, though it undeniably gained him many runs. Having said all that, I had to admire, with countless others, all the Pole B-driven innings that 'Biff' played as a captain leading from the front. His Bradman-like first series in England as a batter (and rookie captain) was unforgettable. South Africa never lost a Test match when he made a century in the fourth innings, and won several. The best examples were the almost-record Perth chase, when he laid the foundation for Kallis, de Villiers and Duminy to finish the job, and the epic undefeated 154 out of 286 at Edgbaston 2008 to take SA to an unlikely win with little help from anybody but Boucher at the end. Smith led an outstanding team, but his own virtues as a batter did much to bring about the South African 'Golden Age' that happened under his watch.

In an earlier SA 'Golden Age', **Graeme Pollock** shared with Smith a first name, a big physique, and an ability to make double centuries with left-handed batting (combined with very occasional right-handed spin); but their batting styles bore little resemblance. Graeme Pollock was one of the princes among left-handers: the adjectives applied to him in his time were 'elegant', 'majestic', 'regal' and the like. (I won't draw comparisons with the similarly described Hashim Amla, because left- and right-handers look too different. For the historically minded, English fans of a certain age compared Pollock in the 1960s with their own tall left-hander of three or four decades before, Frank Woolley, who was said by one writer to belong in a Gainsborough painting.) I was lucky enough to watch Graeme Pollock for well over a decade. At his best, which was most of the time, he didn't need very much footwork. To anything on the off-side, he would simply rock onto either the front or back foot – the only concession he made to the length of the delivery – and lay a heavy bat (bigger than those in general use then) on the ball. The bat's weight, combined with his usually perfect timing, very often sent the ball flashing past fielders before they could move. It all looked so effortless. Fielding captains were often compelled to place a sweeper on the boundary (not the convention it is today), but even that man often couldn't cut off Pollock's drives.

Pollock's leg-side play couldn't quite compare with his off-side dominance, but it was quite adequate: if the bowlers tactically kept it on his legs, he would merely pick off singles and braces while the spectators heckled for more off-side action. And in fact my clearest RGP memory is not of a superb off-side stroke – there were far too many to remember – but one on the leg-side. With Pollock on 95 in a provincial match at the Wanderers (well before lunch after coming in at No. 4, which was the rate he usually scored at), a part-time spinner named Featherstone floated up a head-high full toss, too slow to be called a beamer. Pollock seemed to gently lay a horizontal bat on the ball, which then disappeared onto the scoreboard behind midwicket. A reporter called the stroke a 'nonchalant pull'. Nonchalant, yes; I'm not sure about 'pull', as that stroke usually involves a degree of visible effort and even violence. Graeme Pollock, in this stroke and always, looked effortless and non-violent. His was a rare talent and close to unique.

Allow me one last paragraph here, which goes beyond Graeme Pollock alone to encompass one of his very few left-handed peers, as well as the best of the game's finer feelings. There are countless memorable cricket photographs not actually showing play in progress, the Flintoff-Lee one perhaps standing out. But a personal favourite is from the series between England and the Rest of the World in 1970. Sir Garfield Sobers and Graeme Pollock shared a stand, both making centuries: it must have been the very summit of left-handed batting. In the photo, taken as the two leave the field at stumps, Sobers motions Pollock to pass through the gate first, with Pollock clearly reluctant to do so. The dynamics and context for both men's actions need no explanation. Lucky were the spectators who witnessed the two in the same match, never mind in partnership. An English journalist, sounding more like a reporter of 1870 than 1970, wrote something like "cricket, when played like this, is surely an entertainment for the gods." Even then in the secular twentieth century and more so in the twenty first, it remains hard to disagree.

**Barry Richards** played with classic textbook correctness (rather like Jacques Kallis, but, apart from the physical differences, Richards used his feet much more). Richards managed to score quickly while eliminating risk by adapting his classic technique as required. A good example of this that I saw was when he had to score a boundary in a limited-overs match and received a leg-stump yorker with the leg-side field packed. Richards somehow *double-stepped and backed away to leg simultaneously*, creating space to play a perfect square cover drive to the only available gap. He also departed from the orthodox with a sort of 'pick-up' shot off his legs that often went for six just behind square-leg, not a sweep as he was completely upright; about the only way that a despairing fielding side could get him out when he was set was by placing a fielder there, but he quickly cottoned on to this sort of set-up. Richards seemed to play all his defending and attacking shots with a silky perfection. Watching him was like watching an artist or master craftsman at work. His batting supremacy, long blonde hair, general 'coolness' and surfing habit made him an idol at Durban's Kingsmead. His fellow surfers would often come and watch only until 'Barry freaks out' as they put it. Often they had very long to wait and enjoy.

I will add a BAR story so old it has probably been forgotten. It has been told by too many Australians against themselves for it not to be true. Richards, playing for South against Western Australia in Perth, faced the first ball of a key Sheffield Shield match from Dennis Lillee. He missed it, and WA's original Marsh, the legendary keeper Rodney, tossed the ball to his first slip with the comment, "Thought they said this bloke could bat a bit." Some six hours later, Richards again faced the world's premier pacer for the last ball of the day, ran out to stroke it past Lillee to the sightscreen, and kept on jogging towards the pavilion with his overnight score on 331. The first slip turned to Marsh with total recall, "Guess he can bat a bit." Despite playing only four Tests, Richards was widely recognised as the world's No. 1 batter until he handed the mantle to his namesake Sir Viv in the mid-1970s. The BAR set for later South African batters was a very high one.

**Dudley Nourse** of course retired before most of us were born. But I include him for personal reasons. My father grew up in Durban, and told me tales of how he watched Nourse become the first player to earn the title 'The King of Kingsmead'. (The title was passed on to Roy McLean and then Barry Richards;

Hashim Amla would no doubt have inherited it had he been able to play more often on his home ground.) Nourse came across in my Dad's accounts as a broad-shouldered, rock-like figure at the crease hitting the ball powerfully, especially square on both sides of the wicket off the back foot. This was the first time I heard the description "When he hit the ball, it stayed hit." Others I spoke to who had watched Nourse, as well as what I read, confirmed my father's impressions.

I heard and read much about two of Nourse's innings that stood out – although one of them was immediately upstaged. In his first Test series (at home in 1935/6) he made 231 against the Australian wrist spin trio of Grimmett, O'Reilly and Fleetwood-Smith that otherwise baffled the SA batters for the entire series (with their array of close-in catchers being compared to a multi-armed Hindu god by one fanciful writer). But Stanley McCabe's immediate riposte was an incredible 189 not out (rated as one of three great innings by that Bradman-overshadowed batter) in murky driving rain at Johannesburg's Old Wanderers that apparently hindered the SA fielders more than McCabe, as *their* captain appealed successfully against the conditions. Nourse had no such stealing of his thunder when he made 208 with gritted teeth and a pin in his thumb to set up a win in his first away Test as captain, at Trent Bridge in 1951 (see **Bite 43**). With two such great double-centuries bookending an outstanding career, it was no wonder that Nourse was still talked about reverentially when my interest in cricket began.

(For the record, Faf du Plessis in recent times and Eddie Barlow before isolation would have been my next choices for SA's Magnificent Seven batters. Of current players, Quinton de Kock is an exceptional talent, but not consistent enough, and he left Test cricket prematurely. A final point: Kallis and, not in the same breath, Barlow, as all-rounders are considered in **Part C of this Bite**)

## B. THE MAGNIFICENT SEVEN BOWLERS

**Dale Steyn**'s stellar career is still fresh in the memory. Ali Bacher, who saw every SA quick going back to Adcock and Heine in the 1950s, rates Steyn top of the pile; a Cricinfo analysis found he was the best of all the quicks of his time globally; and it's hard to disagree on either count. As Bacher pointed out, Steyn was virtually the complete fast bowler, with all that he added to the usual pacer's assets: a late outswinger; a command of reverse swing; the fitness/ability to bowl as quickly in the afternoon as the morning; and a fiercely competitive spirit. We all know what the last point referred to – that chain-sawing, forehead vein-throbbing, eye-bulging Viking *berserker* that the normally placid 'Steyntjie' would turn into whenever he took a key wicket; I heard a non-cricket follower remark after glancing at the TV and by chance seeing this spectacle, "Why does that guy suddenly look as if he wants to murder somebody?" Dale will probably be nowhere near that aggressive as he pursues his stated retirement activities of fishing, golf and surfing (with Jonty Rhodes, a near neighbour in Durban). Nobody can grudge him such relatively laid-back leisure after all his successful exertions for South Africa.

**Kagiso Rabada** is my idea of a smart fast bowler. Sure, on a pace-friendly track he can remove batters with the best of them, using his speed, bounce and movement. But watching him go to work on a slower pitch is a treat. He *thinks* the batter out on such tracks (as do most good bowlers, but Rabada stands out), varying quicker with slower balls, inswingers with outswingers, bouncers with yorkers. What the commentators call a three-card trick becomes a four-, five- or six-card trick in his hands; the batter never quite knows what to expect or when. All of this requires a high degree of accuracy, which Rabada has; the end result is a bowler who is as valuable bowling the final over an IPL innings as the first over of a Test. 'K.G.' is also a perfectly built athlete whose lissom grace has been described as gazelle-like. The old cliché of 'poetry in motion' applies to him as much as to any cricketer. The prospect of watching him lead SA's attack in all formats for several more seasons is one to relish.

**Vernon Philander** may seem a sudden reduction in pace in this company, but opposing batters made that assumption at their peril. There was a reason for South Africa pairing Philander with Steyn up front, rather than the third member of the dominant pace trio of the time, Morne Morkel. Though perhaps no more than fast-medium, Philander could be lethal with the new ball, especially earlier in his career. He pitched most balls where the batter had to play it, and he seemed to have an uncanny ability to move the 'cherry' the exact amount required, either way, to find the edge or slip it just past the edge onto the pad. He was most dangerous bowling from over the wicket across left-handers, unleashing the one that reversed direction and cut back into them for a likely LBW. He made short work of the England left-handed opening pair of Cook and Strauss in this way more than once. Philander was sometimes nicknamed 'Vern McGrath' by his teammates: I think the comparison with Australia's great Glenn was based not only on a common relentless accuracy, but the sheer difficulty that openers had in not getting out in the early overs against either of them.

**Makhaya Ntini:** It was hard to put a finger, technically, on exactly why Ntini was so successful: from the ring, he didn't seem to quite command the pace, variation or movement that his figures suggested. His whippy action wasn't a classic one. Yet he had a way of apparently rushing batters into mistakes, almost 400 of them in Tests. I have a theory from watching him a great deal that *he actually gained pace off the pitch.* It was said of the great England post-war spearhead, Alec Bedser, that he seemed to be fast-medium through the air but then fast off the pitch; I had the same impression of Ntini. You can argue forever about all the physics and optics involved, but it was what the batters experienced that counted. Ntini's fairy-tale rise from a dusty rural village via elite school to the international arena came at exactly the right time for South Africa; just what the doctor (Bacher) ordered. I hesitate to add 'politically speaking', as that would suggest some kind of expediency about his selection, whereas it was infinitely justified on merit. It was sad to read that he felt lonely in the Proteas off-field setup and would even run between the hotel and stadium to avoid sitting alone in the team bus. As far as I could judge from the stands, on the field his boundless and bubbly joy in the game was infectious and made him the heart of the team's enthusiasm. And I never saw anything but displays of affection from his team-mates for 'Makkie'.

**Shaun Pollock** was generally called 'Polly', but at times and often by opponents, the 'Ginger Ninja'. The red hair, not inherited from either his father Peter or uncle Graeme, is supposed to go with a quick temper, but that wasn't the case with him. The two nicknames somehow summed up the contrast between his affable personality at most times and his fierce resolve when he had the bit between his teeth and the ball (or bat) in hand (a contrast similar to that found in Dale Steyn and other friendly/furious fast bowlers, but it seemed especially marked in Pollock). As a bowler he made maximum use of his height, bowling a good deal just 'back of a length' (his own words) to get enough bounce to keep the batter uncomfortable without allowing him an easy back-foot shot. A ball pitched further up would sometimes cut in sharply as well, often surprising the batter. Pollock was an exceptionally loyal servant of SA cricket, taking over the captaincy uncomplainingly when the Cronje thunderbolt burst out of the blue.

**Allan Donald** was dubbed 'White Lightning' and even called his autobiography that, but you have to be South African to realise there was more to the nickname than his light colouring and pace. The Afrikaans translation, *Witblits,* carries the same connotations (think of the German Blitzkrieg of World War Two), but can also refer to a moonshine liquor, often made from peaches, that can be up to seventy per cent proof on a bad/good day. The idea was that Donald gave batters a similar headache (sometimes literally – it probably wasn't the wisest thing he ever did, when the UAE's Sultan Zarawani came out to face him in a sunhat, to 'ping' the Emirati for showing disrespect – see **Bite 45**). Donald's express pace was probably the main factor in most of his wickets. Of course he wouldn't have defeated so many good batters without some movement as well. Few will forget the blistering off-cutter that whistled through Sachin Tendulkar's near-impregnable defence in a Test at the Wanderers, or Donald's Boeing celebration that followed (South African Airways, a more viable concern then than in recent times, even borrowed the footage for an advert).

Fast bowlers often hunt best in pairs, as history shows; Donald was fortunate to have the combative seamer Fanie de Villiers as a partner, and later Shaun Pollock in what was surely one of South Africa's finest new-ball pairings. Somebody once wrote of Donald and Pollock sharing the England wickets on a pace-friendly pitch that they tore into the batters like two hungry predators on a carcass: two lions savaging the Three Lions?

**Mike Procter** in full cry was one of the most thrilling sights of the immediate pre-isolation era. He had the longest run-up I've ever seen, starting perhaps two-thirds of the way to the sight screen, and would have cost his captain plenty for slow over rates today. But the crowds didn't mind it then: every Procter ball was a spectacle. The anticipation built up by the second as the powerful fair-haired figure thundered in, reached the crease going flat out, and released with his explosive, apparently wrong-footed action. At his high pace there shouldn't have been much swing, but there was, perhaps a product of that unusual action: nearly every ball was a 'banana ', curving in like a swiftly flung frisbee or boomerang. He didn't have an outswinger that I could see, perhaps because he didn't need one: he achieved the same effect by making the odd ball hold its line, instead of the usual sharp swerve that the batter was expecting (see **Bite 16** on how he outfoxed the canny left-handed Australian opener Lawry in this way). Procter formed one of those formidable pace pairs with Peter Pollock, and he was also in a very rare class of all-rounder, as I argue in **Bite 19**.

(This list would have very probably have included Vintcent (*correct spelling*) van der Bijl if fate had allowed 'Big Vince' a Test career. The balding gentle giant spearheaded Natal's attack for many years before he ended his career going north to Transvaal and further north to Middlesex, contributing significantly to both teams winning domestic championships in the early 80s. When Middlesex lifted the county trophy in 1981, a London headline dubbed him 'Van der Champion".)

### C. THE MAGNIFICENT SEVEN ALL-ROUNDERS
All-rounders have been a hallmark of South African teams

over the years; possibly more so than with any other country, though Australia might dispute this. I will single out six of them; at least four would qualify as 'genuine' by the traditional definition.

**Jacques Kallis** must count as the country's greatest ever all-rounder on sheer weight of Test runs, reflected in his exceptional century count, plus Test wickets. Kallis's batting was classically executed, as seen in **part A of this Bite**; the same could be said of his penetrating fast-medium bowling. Perhaps the best acknowledgement of this actually came in a coaching video made by a frequent opponent, Andrew Flintoff. The England all-rounder demonstrated most of the batting and seam bowling techniques himself, justifiably. But when it came to the outswinger/leg-cutter, he chose to show Kallis gripping the ball and then delivering it in the perfect way to make the ball move out, square up the batter and take the outside edge – that batter being, in a very 'Freddie' bit of self-deprecation, Flintoff himself! Kallis was also more than accurate enough to dry up the runs in white-ball matches and hardly missed a catch at second slip, his frequent position, or anywhere else.

**Lance Klusener** is remembered today mainly as a limited-overs 'finisher' of note and power: as someone who would walk in to the chant of "Zulu! Zulu!" (from home crowds at least, referring to his farm upbringing-derived fluency in that language) with his side needing plenty of runs per over, and would club a string of sixes to get them over the line. This perception is unjust to his Test record. He started in meteoric fashion with a century and an *eight*-for in his 1996 maiden series in India of all places; and continued to perform consistently. His batting might have achieved greater heights if he hadn't come in as low as 8 or 9 so often; as it was, he often had to bat against his instincts to save a game. As a bowler he was a bustling fast-medium, but so aggressive that he could seem fast (much like Botham or Flintoff). It's often forgotten today that Klusener could also slow down to medium pace and bowl sharp off-cutters (watching his fingers carefully, I thought a few were actually off-*spinners*) with the keeper standing up; this gave his captains a very useful option on the subcontinent in particular, especially with a left-arm spinner at the other end. Across formats, he was just a few years ahead of his time. Imagine that six-hitting and those pace variations in the death overs of a T20 match; and imagine the telephone numbers that Lance Klusener might have attracted at an IPL auction!

**Shaun Pollock** may have put just a little too much focus on his exemplary bowling. He never made quite as many runs as he might have with his talent (and genes), but he was a very reliable batter in the middle order. He did score two Test centuries, plus a third in a would-be Test against India at Centurion that the ICC declared unofficial. As a white-ball power hitter he was once required to out-Brathwaite Brathwaite: Carlos hit his four straight sixes when he had a whole over to make merely 20 off the luckless Stokes, but Shaun's only winning option was to take each of the last four balls for the maximum in an ODI in New Zealand. Pollock cleared the boundary three times before a relieved Kyle Mills found the right length to thwart a fourth. Shaun Pollock will go down as a bowling all-rounder and very close to a genuine one.

**Mike Procter**, Shaun's father's Test new-ball partner, was, for me, South Africa's No. 2 all-time all-rounder just behind Kallis. It is hard to see anyone emulating Kallis' all-round achievements, but Procter might have, given a full Test career. He was a very rare breed of cricketer, as argued in **Bite 19**.

It's rare for an opening batter to double up as one of the mainstays of his team's attack. **Trevor Goddard**, one of my earliest heroes (along with Graeme Pollock), filled this unusual dual role. Goddard, left-handed in both disciplines, was an automatic choice as opening batter when available for almost fifteen years, forming part of two successive SA 'Old Firms' with Jackie McGlew and then Eddie Barlow. Oddly, he took ten of those years to make his maiden Test century, despite scoring enough 80s and 90s to keep his place secure. I was watching my very first day of Test cricket as a nine-year-old when Goddard pushed one past gully off an England bowler at the Wanderers to reach the milestone (adding still further to my childish satisfaction was that my father had taken me out of school for the occasion). As a bowler, Goddard must have varied his pace Lohmann-like over a wide range, as he was regularly first change or occasionally took the new ball, and yet wicket-keepers sometimes stood up to the stumps for him. One of those keepers, Denis Lindsay, when asked what Goddard was doing, replied, "Trevor's swinging them in circles". Goddard was never dropped until after what proved to be his last Test, the Third in the clean sweep over Australia in 1970, and then it was made clear that he would have played in the fourth match had the series still been at stake. He has been described as one of the most underrated of all-rounders.

**Eddie Barlow**, mentioned above, doesn't really belong in this company, but he was and remains, for me and many who watched him, irresistible. Other words like rumbunctious, ebullient and exuberant were used by reporters to describe him, while his opponents often used shorter words. Today we would call him 'feisty'. He scored heavily in Tests as an opener for a decade, mostly alongside Goddard. His bowling at barely fast-medium was greatly boosted by a huge self-belief that saw him often persuade his captain to hand him the ball and then 'burgle' a wicket or two; today we might say he had a 'Golden Arm'. Barlow and Goddard must be among the few pairs to have opened both the batting and bowling in the same Test, as once happened in Australia. Barlow's early death, like Clive Rice's, deprived South African cricket of a definite character.

**Aubrey Faulkner:** Obviously I never saw Faulkner, but statistics show him to be among the leading all-rounders ever, and the best batter/wrist-spinner among them (the multifaceted Sobers aside). Faulkner's outstanding batting allowed South Africa to field a formidable quartet of leg-spinners, as noticed in **Bite 35**. My favourite Faulkner story, courtesy of Neville Cardus, is from the twilight of his playing career, as well as that of the iconic English Test captain/administrator, Lord 'Archie' McLaren. The 1921 Australians were set to end their tour of England undefeated, as would their post-war counterparts, the 'Invincibles', twenty-seven years later. McLaren said he could pick and lead a team to beat these Australians. Without residential restrictions, he chose Faulkner (who happened to be in England at the time) as the imported warhead in a mostly amateur side. The great South African duly obliged, making 153 in a low-scoring match to help 'A.C. McLaren's XI' spoil the Australian side's unbeaten record – the final highlight of Faulkner's distinguished career.

### D. THE MAGNIFICENT TWO FIELDERS
(*A Tale of Two Run-Outs*)

The commentators of two different eras said it all, more by their tone than words. "Jonty Rhodes has demolished the stumps!" Mike Haysman's startled yelp conveyed the astonishment that we all felt at the now iconic run-out we had just seen on TV. More long-winded than Haysman, the pre-TV radio commentator Charles Fortune described a run-out by an earlier fielding genius as follows: "And they trot through for an easy single... (*then Charles' languid tone suddenly took on a frenzied excitement*) No! There's an appeal and Barrington is out, run out! Bland has swooped like an eagle and hit the wicket!" I promise you he actually did say 'like an eagle' in the midst of the uproar. That snatch of commentary, vintage Charles (see **Bite 16**), has stuck in my memory. But this is about **Colin Bland** and **Jonty Rhodes**; I'll talk about the more recent of the two 'uber-fielders' first.

**Jonty's** dive onto the stumps to run out Inzamam ul-Haq at South Africa's first World Cup became an instant sensation. The photo was on the front page of the most serious newspapers, not just in SA. Young schoolboys tried to imitate it and their coaches had to warn them that the stump spikes could hurt them. The image even appeared on a set of five-rand coins brought out by the South African Mint. Rhodes himself is said to have given two explanations for the extraordinary play. One was that he could get the ball onto the stumps and break them faster that way; the other and more likely was a quote from him: "I'd been missing the stumps with my throws recently, so I wanted to make sure."

Be that as it may, the dive was typical, vintage Jonty. He seemed almost to be able to fly when he threw himself sideways or upwards to pluck a catch in mid-air. His favourite position was at backward point, but he could field anywhere and bring off catches that few other players could have managed. I remember a rather wordy headline in an Indian newspaper after Rhodes had caught five Windies batters in a single innings, only one a routine catch: "RHODES' ATHLETICISM FELLS WEST INDIES".

'Athleticism' was almost an understatement: he moved at times like an Olympics gymnast or a trapeze artist. His ground fielding was also a marvel of gathering the ball and releasing it in what seemed a single motion. From there his throw would often hit the stumps: he ran out many batters by more orthodox means than the Inzamam stump-smashing. Jonty was probably worth 50-60 runs to his side in a typical fielding innings, in terms not only of runs cut off but also quick runs declined by batters who knew his reputation.

The reaction to one Bradman dismissal seemed to foreshadow Jonty Rhodes, at least as described by Neville Cardus, who was there at Lord's in 1930 (see **Bite 31**). A spectator asked why Bradman was leaving the field. He was asked if he'd missed that wonderful catch by the England captain Chapman in the gully. He replied, according to Cardus, *"What proof is there that the ball Chapman threw up was the same one that left Bradman's bat?"* The sceptical spectator (who was author James Barrie; perhaps he saw some Peter Pan-like unreality in the catch) didn't mean that there'd been any sharp practice, of course; merely that it had all happened too fast to comprehend and believe. Many of Jonty's catches were like that.

**Colin Bland** was equally magical in his own way, as far as I could tell with limited opportunities to watch him in pre-TV days in South Africa and when I was young. Even at school we talked about Bland as the gold standard for fielding, passing on what we heard from parents, teachers and coaches. The commentators, as I recall, went all poetic with their comparisons: Charles Fortune called Bland a swooping eagle, as we saw; the BBC's John Arlott made him a panther pouncing. What I remember seeing for myself was the way Bland sometimes warmed up before play began. He would take a number of cricket balls out with him and fire them at a single stump from about 40 metres. He hit it perhaps eight times out of ten. I recall how fans watched in fascination as the stump sagged further over every time it was struck; sometimes Bland knocked it out of the ground and his assistant had to replace it. So that lightning accuracy of his throws came from hard work and practice as well as a natural talent.

Bland usually fielded at cover (so not the same position as Jonty, but the classic post at the time for a side's best fielder) in an era when it was less common than later to have a 'sweeper' on the off-side boundary. He must have seemed to the batter like a wall or a barrier blocking off that boundary: a drive or cut would have to be hit powerfully and probably a good ten or 15 metres away from him to get through. Nobody dared to risk a quick single to Bland; sometimes when it seemed an easy single, the batters did set off, but then they often suffered Barrington's fate. If Rhodes in the field was worth 50+ per innings to his side in runs saved or declined, Bland may have accounted for even more, if you bear in mind that without a sweeper, many of the strokes he intercepted would have been fours.

I should add that both Rhodes and Bland were always worth their place in the SA team as batters. The figures make this clear for both of them, and I think the last time specialist fielders were chosen for a side was in the Victorian era when fields could still be bumpy. (One such player, the Rev Vernon Royle, was said to have been as handy in the covers as in the chancel; many a fielder has done superb work while down on his knees.)

There have of course many great fielders in cricket history; and with the demands of white-ball formats, much higher fielding standards are required of all players today. How exceptional were Rhodes and Bland? A video analyst prepared to spend half a lifetime on the project, and with total access to all the game's vast store of film and TV archival footage, could no doubt determine the globally most efficient fielder since the technology became available (sadly excluding earlier figures like Rev Royle) in terms of runs saved and wickets taken via catches and run-outs. The analyst might come up with a contemporary fielding star, perhaps Ravi Jadeja; an earlier one like Ricky Ponting or before him the great West Indies captain Clive Lloyd; or one from the black-and-white footage days like Neil Harvey. England's Sir Jack Hobbs once ran out Bradman with a direct hit from cover when Hobbs was aged forty-six; one can imagine how the greatest English batter had fielded when he was younger. Most of the statistician's possible candidates generally fielded at cover, but cricket has changed.

But these Bites are about impressions, not stats. Jonty Rhodes and Colin Bland both had an aura of legend about them that set them apart from all other fielders, at least South African, in my experience of cricket. That is why I have opted to single out only two fielders, not seven, and given them so much space. This particular Hall of Fame is a tiny room.

# 38. SOUTH AFRICAN AND OTHER 'DYNASTIES'
## (*Of fathers, sons, grandsons and a mercenary*)

The newly arrived South African professional had scarcely unpacked his bags when he was invited to be one of the guests of honour at a charity gala dinner in Northampton, England. The MC of the event hadn't a clue who the cricket newcomer was when the time came to introduce him. So a whispered question was hastily passed along the prominent sports people sitting along the High Table: "Where exactly do you come from?" The whispered reply was relayed back to the MC, "A place between Hamburg and Berlin." The MC looked a little puzzled, but then collected himself and announced to the assembled guests, "And last but not least, ladies and gentlemen, we welcome Herr Hylton Ackermann from somewhere in Germany!"

This story must be true, because it was told to the South African Cricket Society twice by the two best possible sources: the late Hylton Ackerman (spelt with one N) himself, and then repeated some twenty years later by his son, also named Hylton, but generally known as 'H.D.' to differentiate him. (The father had grown up in the Eastern Cape's Border region, where a number of towns were settled by former German mercenaries in the British Army and named accordingly.)

The two Ackermans were one of South Africa's better

father-and-son cricket pairs. Hylton Senior would certainly have played for SA but for isolation. As it was, he starred as a top-order batter for as many as four South African provinces, for Northants – presumably after clearing up that initial confusion about his nationality – and for the Rest of the World XI against Australia in 1971/2, opening the ROW innings with no less than Sunil Gavaskar. 'H.D.' won the Test cap that had eluded his father and also followed him into county cricket, playing for Leicestershire as a batting mainstay. Both had a great sense of humour and relished telling the "Herr Ackermann" story.

The lifelong cricket fan who watches the same home team for long enough has a good chance of feeling that 'dynastic' sense of recognition sooner or later. News reports and the Cricinfo website will probably tell you well in advance that a former player's son has now been selected for the local team. But you still have the fun of looking for the poses, mannerisms and aspects of playing style that you were familiar with in the father. My most vivid personal experience of this came when Stephen Cook and Neil McKenzie started playing for the Gauteng Lions, formerly Transvaal: their fathers Jimmy and Kevin had made bundles of runs for the Transvaal 'Mean Machine' of the 80s (Jimmy also for Somerset, including a triple century). Stephen is one of the handful of SA players to make a century on Test debut; Neil has a share in the world record Test opening stand at the time of writing; Jimmy was one of the oldest Test debutants. Kevin was exceptional in another way, personally for me, as related in **Bite 44.**

The supreme South African cricket 'dynasty', though, has to be the Pollock family. Shaun was a fast bowler of the same calibre as his father Peter; and I once read a report on one of Shaun's best batting efforts saying that he'd looked at times like a right-handed version of his uncle Graeme – perhaps far-fetched, but Shaun was certainly a batter to fear at his best. Graeme's sons Anthony and Andrew only played sporadically for Transvaal; and Shaun has 'only' daughters (apologies for the word 'only'; I've watched for the name in Proteas women's team mix, so far in vain). But a sharp eye will be kept on all their descendants. There are parallels for a 'skipped generation' in other countries. Australia's great brothers Ian and Greg Chappell are the grandsons of a highly respected 1920s captain, Vic Richardson; I'll come to another example shortly.

There are too many of these families in world cricket to talk about here. I'll mention two based in England with strong Southern African connections. Kevin Curran was a forceful all-rounder for Zimbabwe and Natal before his move to England and early death; his sons are Sam, Tom and the lesser known Ben, still playing at the county level as I write. And two more D'Oliveira generations of Worcestershire county players have already followed Basil, whose move to England to escape apartheid restrictions had such huge repercussions: son Damian and grandson Brett.

It is of course unfair and an unnecessary burden to expect too much of the son of a high-achieving father. Cricket has perhaps the best example in all sport: John Bradman/Bradsen hardly played the game, but he was so hounded by expectations and undue attention that he eventually changed the most hallowed surname in Australia (he did reclaim it in later life). In other cases the son has performed at a high level, but short of the father's heights; Richard Hutton and Chris Cowdrey both played for England without achieving the rarefied distinction of Sir Leonard and Lord Colin.

Without name-dropping, I had an interesting personal

insight into the son's typical feelings in these cases. Richard Compton was at university in Pietermaritzburg with me; he remarked once, "Thank goodness my dad moved to South Africa; not so many people here have heard of him." However, Richard's son Nick has played for England and his nephew Ben may yet do so, after his prolific start for Kent in 2022. Richard and his brother Patrick, Ben's father, both had only brief first-class careers, so the Compton line also more or less 'skipped a generation'. As to inherited talent, Nick and Ben both come across as workmanlike openers, lacking the prototype-'Mr 360' brilliance of their grandfather Denis; but few batters possess that in any era.

Lastly, I can't resist mentioning the Mann clan's African sorties over three generations, though only two involved cricket. F.T. Mann captained the England/MCC side in South Africa in 1921/2. His son F.G. (George) Mann led England/MCC in SA in 1948/9 (when his dismissal by the home side's 'Tufty' Mann prompted the all-time commentator's classic noted in **Bite 14**). Despite this lineage, George's son Simon didn't play any significant cricket. Instead his African mission was as a mercenary (with SAS training) leading the farcical 2004 botched coup in Equatorial Guinea, reportedly funded by Mark Thatcher's "splodge of wonka" and apparently based on Frederick Forsyth's novel *The Dogs of War* as an instruction manual. Languishing in a pestilential EG jail for years, Simon may have reflected that his father and grandfather had been in only slightly less unenviable positions as England cricket captains, perennial Press whipping-boys.

By his own admission, though, Simon Mann was never good enough at cricket to have completed a family generational triple, only ever achieved by the Headleys of West Indies/England and the Khans of India/Pakistan. (So if Simon *had* been good enough, the Manns would have been the only such trio to have all played for the same Test nation. Jahangir Khan, who played for India pre-Partition in 1936, is somehow remembered less for founding a Test-playing line than for bowling a delivery that hit and killed a sparrow at Lord's, still preserved there complete with the ball.)

The whole idea of 'dynasties' and hereditary entitlement is very much out of fashion today. Much of the media do their best to trash the British royal family, to say nothing of the mostly fictional soapie *The Crown*. But when it comes to inherited natural talent emerging in a sport, the notion of 'dynasty' still grips us whenever we see a familiar surname. Cricket has a number of families with the potential to yield the proverbial apples falling close to their tree or chips off the old block. Fans will continue to feel the thrill of recognising a player's surname, confirming his heredity, and then seeing it manifested on the field.

## 39. SOUTH AFRICAN GROUNDS: OUTSIDE THE GRANDSTANDS
### (*SA grounds' non-stand areas - grass, oaks, beach sand, beer, banter and barracking*)

Cricket stadiums (or 'stadia' if you prefer) these days are comfortable places: generally every seat around the ground is plastic. No longer do you have to bring a cushion (or buy one from enterprising vendors outside the ground) or risk your fleshier parts on hard wooden benches. These were not well maintained near the scoreboard at the Wanderers Stadium in the past: those who sat there were dubbed the 'splinter group.'

But parts of some grounds do not, or did not, even have seats. These are the areas where spectators come if they want to relax, recline on the ground, enjoy the sun and often have *braais* (barbecues), washed down with beer in mandatory plastic cups. Along with this goes much banter, not all of it cricket-related. Watching the cricket from these areas has a particular flavour and 'vibe' not found in the grandstands. I'll describe some of these areas at various South African grounds.

The New **Wanderers** still has such an area, known as the Grass Enclosure (sometimes Embankment). It's just below the pavilion and slopes down next to the gangway used by the players to enter and leave the field. During my first years of cricket-watching at the Wanderers, I never sat anywhere else. My hero-worship of the players was such that I just wanted to watch them going up and down the steps, often seeking their autographs along with scores of other cricket-mad schoolboys. I also enjoyed the banter of adult fans, while ignoring the coarser language, as I'd been taught to do.

What the Grass Enclosure did not offer was what I might call 'the purist's angle' on the game. This is, of course, a view from behind the stumps at either end, up and down the pitch, allowing the spectator to watch what the ball is doing. The Grass Enclosure is square on. That was why, as I came to better appreciate the subtleties of the game, I moved to the more edifying angles from the grandstands and the company of sterner spectators – though not without a certain wistful envy when I looked across at the fun going on in my former habitat.

But that clash of priorities was perfectly eliminated when **Supersport Park** came into being in Centurion just outside Pretoria, some 40 km to the north of the Wanderers. Whoever designed Supersport knew what a traditional village cricket ground looked like and was determined to keep some of its flavour even in an international stadium set amongst dense development and a busy freeway. The 'Grass Embankment' here (it's not even enclosed) has a distinct village feel, but unlike the one at the Wanderers, it's actually next to the sightscreen at one end. So you have the best of both worlds – a 'purist's view' of the play combined with grassy surroundings.

So you can enjoy a hard-fought Test match or ODI at Supersport while relaxing in a sort of village festival atmosphere of deck-chairs, blankets, picnics and *braai*'s (barbecues), usually in the sun or on a balmy evening in the case of day-night matches.

The tone is a sort of jovial-serious, somewhere between the extremes of the grandstand and the Grass Enclosure at the Wanderers. Cricket spectatorship can hardly offer a better all-senses experience than watching a top-flight match from this part of Supersport Park.

**Newlands** in Cape Town used to have an equivalent area that was part of cricket and cultural folklore, known as 'Under the Oaks'. The tall stately trees lent an ambience that was somehow redolent of both cricket and the Mother City - graceful, elegant, time-honoured. The very phrase 'Under the Oaks' conveyed part of the Cape Town experience; it often appeared in newspapers and sports magazines, and even in the title of a drama by the popular South African playwright Paul Slabolepszy.

I didn't manage to get down to the Cape and Newlands during the Oaks enclosure's halcyon days very often: but when I did, I felt almost duty bound to sit there. The angle for watching the cricket was adequate if not perfect, behind long-off and fine-leg (for a right-hander). The level of knowledge among the fans, as well as the flashes of humour, seemed to me to be more elevated than that found in the brasher cities up-country. I was sad when I came back to Newlands after most of the Oaks had disappeared in the interests of revamping the stadium for the post-isolation era. But at least there was still the eternal spectacle of Table Mountain looming above the stands, often propping up a clear blue sky in bright sunshine. When these conditions are present, there can hardly be a more beautiful setting for cricket in the world (though see at the end of this Bite.)

**Kingsmead** in Durban had a very different set of attractions when I went there regularly during student days. The open area there was quite explicit about the type of fan it attracted. It was called 'Castle Corner', after a brand of beer popular in South

Africa ever since one Charles Glass created it in 1895 (the same year of Lord Hawke's cricket tour and the Jameson Raid – it's interesting to ponder which of these three English initiatives had the most lasting effect on the country's future). Often clutching a can of the namesake beverage, you sat on very patchy grass amid what was essentially beach sand, as the Indian Ocean shoreline was only some 500 metres away.

This location caused me to indulge in an extra jaunt which very few cricket fans, if any, can have shared with me. During the forty or forty-five minutes of the lunch interval, I just had time to run to the stadium exit, grab a 'Passout' ticket from the usher, run to North Beach, splash into the surf and catch a wave or two (bodysurfing, of course) and run back to Kingsmead and Castle Corner in time for the first ball after the break. This may sound crazy to you, but students do such zany things, and the sensory pleasures of these aquatic interludes only heightened the joy of a day at the cricket. These remain among my best cricket memories.

**The banter and repartee** in all these areas was highly entertaining, as was the related heckling – or 'barracking' as it used to be known – directed at the players, especially the boundary fielders only metres away. Not much of it would sound terribly amusing now in cold hard print; you had to be there to find it funny. But I will recall three memorable utterances.

One piece of intricate wordplay from a fan remains with me from my very first day of live Test cricket, partly because it was in Afrikaans and my father had to translate and explain. South Africa's No. 3 at the time, Tony Pithey, was crawling along at a pace that drove even the Wanderers home crowd to slow-handclap him (a discourteous habit that has since disappeared, partly because even Test batting is seldom slow in the present era). Pithey may have set a career-determining example to a new young England opener in the field that day in 1964, named Geoff Boycott.

It happened that the series had been marred by some acrimony between the two sides over batters 'walking' or not (a frequent controversy before DRS). An Afrikaans fan in the Grass Enclosure captured all of this by yelling, "*Pithey, jy moet nou óf hardloop óf loop!*" This translates as "Pithey, now you must either run or walk!", rather lame in English, but in Afrikaans it contains a verbal echo that makes it much cleverer (which would have been as lost on Pithey, a Rhodesian, as Hindi heckling is on non-Indian players today).

Australian 'boundary riders' were naturally a particular target for the Saffer jibes. Jason Gillespie was once snubbing all the schoolboys trying to reach over the Wanderers Grass Enclosure barriers with their pens and autograph books and get him to sign (rightly so, of course; no fielder should let himself be so distracted from the play in the middle). Somebody shouted, "Don't worry, Jason, you're allowed to sign with an X!" Gillespie gave one quick signature at the end of the session, disproving the slur on his literacy (everyone wanted to see the lucky schoolboy's miniature bat).

David 'Keg on Legs' Boon (he of the walrus moustache and record number of beers consumed on the Sydney-London Ashes flight) was being chaffed by Grass Enclosure fans about the reputed habits of his countrymen in the Outback. He turned to face them and replied, "You blokes have got it all wrong. It's the Kiwis who shag sheep, not us." There were apparently no New Zealanders present in the Enclosure to take up this interesting trans-Tasman debate, to the disappointment of the assembled Saffers.

So what future is there in twenty first century cricket for these egregious enclosures and the witty spectator comments they engender? The absolute cricket aficionado will perhaps sit nowhere but a grandstand, wanting to concentrate exclusively on the play without distractions. Many other spectators, however, have come to enjoy both the play and the vibrancy of the crowd atmosphere. They will continue to sit in the areas where the latter is most felt.

Sadly, the classic comment shouted for the entire ground to hear is much rarer today, at least in South Africa. The individual spectator with a gift for shouted witticisms has almost disappeared. There were a few regulars with this gift in the enclosures I frequented in SA. (None of these, admittedly, would have had a statue erected to him, like the one at Australia's SCG honouring Yabba the legendary arch-barracker, the acerbic player-heckling king of the Sydney Hill.) But the occasional pearl of wit or wisdom can and does still issue forth from the fans. And one advantage of the modern era is that it if another fan is quick enough, it could be captured on somebody's smartphone and go viral for the enjoyment of the entire cricket community.

(A quick parenthesis on my favourite grounds overseas. **Lord**'s, for reasons that don't need explaining. **Eden Gardens** in Kolkata, for that 'seething cauldron' effect produced when 100,000 of some of the world's most passionate fans are crowded together. And **Galle** in Sri Lanka, not for the stadium itself, but for the panoramic views the camera regularly gives of the old Portuguese-Dutch fort, the harbour, the beach and the translucent sea plied by fishing vessels and passenger cruisers. This setting may admittedly rival and even surpass that of Newlands, as may the ground at **Dharamsala** with its Himalayan backdrop.)

# 40. MY FAVOURITE SOUTH AFRICAN MATCHES

(*I preface each of these five matches with my reasons for choosing it, posed mostly as bracketed questions. The four Tests were all matches I followed very closely – in the case of the earliest one, either on radio as SA didn't have TV then, or watching live at the Wanderers as an entranced schoolboy. I plead not guilty to possible charges of Saffer chauvinism, citing that I do include one SA defeat with the three victories. I've chosen only one interprovincial match out of the scores that I've watched, because of its sheer enjoyment factor at the time, which I explain.*)

### A. South Africa vs Sri Lanka, Durban, 2019

*(Did this Test see the greatest individual Test innings played in South Africa, or, as has been argued, even more than that? Was it also the Test match of the 2010s decade, as has also been argued?)*

It was arguably also the biggest Test match upset ever seen in South Africa, and it was mainly down to Kusal Perera.

First, there was the wider context. Sri Lanka, formidable opponents on their own island, had never seriously threatened to win a series in South Africa. Their bevy of great or near-great – batters – Jayasuriya, Attapatu, Sangakkara and more – had never made quite enough of their runs on SA, nor had Muralidharan taken enough of his 800 Test wickets there. The touring team of early 2019 contained no names like these and was not expected to break the pattern. The home side's attack pace trio, with Duanne Olivier suddenly emerging as a fearsome quick alongside Steyn and Rabada. The trio had just blown away a strong Pakistan batting line-up, with even Babar Azam fending catches off rearing short balls, at the speedsters' happy hunting grounds of the Wanderers, Supersport Park and Newlands. Even on the slower track at Kingsmead, the pace attack plus Philander and Maharaj were expected to dispose of this SL team.

The Durban pitch indeed seemed to give the home quicks less help than the visiting swing bowlers, and Vishwa Fernando especially kept the SA batting in check. He could not have known what an important part he still had to play in the match. Sri Lanka had to make 304 to win, a higher total than had been achieved in the match. Perera looked determined and in good form, but at 228 for nine, the rest seemed to be a formality. SA seemed to grow a little complacent and perhaps did too little to get the same Vishwa, the last man, on strike.

As time went on it became clear Perera was doing much more than that: he was playing a rare masterclass of an innings. As the SA bowlers stepped up their efforts on a sluggish pitch now helping neither ball nor bat, he mixed solid defence with powerful attacking strokes. His eventual ratio of five sixes to 12 fours was high for a Test match, even in the twenty first century. The target drew steadily closer, as the tension grew and the improbable gradually became the likely outcome. With 11 to get, Perera hit one from Steyn in the 'slot' for his last six, deftly retained the strike and finished the match by guiding Rabada to the third man boundary.

I think I can honestly say that most Saffer fans, despite the shock and disappointment, appreciated what an extraordinary innings Kusal Perera had played. He had passed 150 in a low-scoring match; he had made almost all of the 86 required for the last wicket, while preserving his wicket and his partner's; everybody, including ardent South African fans, admired the enormous courage and skill that went into this. I think most rated Perera's innings as a better one than the very similar feat by Stokes at Headingley a few months earlier.

So was it the greatest Test innings played in South Africa? Data analyst Anantha Naranayan has actually pronounced it the best Test innings *anywhere* in a Cricinfo article, using about 10 quantifiable parameters. Whatever your criteria, Perera's innings has to be up there, especially if you give weight to a batter striving alone with little support.

**(***Way off topic, but allow me to add here a fascinating titbit about cricket contact between South Africans and Sri Lankans before either country existed in the forms we know today. It fits in better here than anywhere else in my Bites and is too interesting to leave out. Ceylon, as Sri Lanka was formerly known, was one of the places where the British Army deported Boer prisoners during the Anglo-Boer /South African War. There is a record of Boer POW's in Ceylon playing a cricket match against a local XI. The scorecard shows that a bowler named P. de Villiers took five wickets, anticipating the overseas successes of P.S. 'Fanie' de Villiers by almost a century.***)**

### B. South Africa vs Australia, Newlands, 2011

*(Has a debutant bowler ever turned his maiden Test around like this?)*

You had to feel for Australian captain Michael Clarke. On a Newlands pitch that helped both sides' strong pace-seam attacks for the first two days, he was the only batter to cope, and that superbly. Clarke made 151 out for 284 and then saw his bowlers sweep the home team away for 96. Yet his side's advantage vanished like the 'table-cloth' cloud on nearby Table Mountain as the batters, Clarke included, could scarcely middle a ball and tumbled to *21 for nine* in the second innings. New Zealand's record low Test score of 26 was in distinct danger. Several Kiwi feedbackers to Cricinfo expressed disappointment as the last-wicket pair of Siddle and Lyon spared the worst of Australia's blushes – but not much else, as the final total of 47 was still a 109-year low for them. The pitch eased on the third day and Graeme Smith and Hashim Amla seemed to be playing in a different match as they coasted to a target of 236, both making centuries.

Half the visitors' wickets in that extraordinary third innings fell to a Test debutant named Vernon Philander, a Capetonian who was picked because he'd been doing so well on his home ground. Whether it was his knowledge of the Newlands track, or because the Australians hadn't yet come to grips with his knack of pitching each ball in exactly the right place and finding the exact amount of movement needed to dislodge each batter (see **Bite 37B**), they had no answers.

Philander's 5/15 in his second Test innings as a bowler (on top of 3/63 in the first, when he took time to settle to Test cricket) fails to make the first page of the list of Best Figures on Test Debut, which is replete with eight-, seven- and six-fors. I believe his contribution was as valuable as most of those above him, for three reasons. Firstly, his experienced pace colleagues, Steyn and Morne Morkel, benefited from the panic sown by this deadly new bowler to scalp the other five of the harried Australian batters in the second innings. Second, Philander's miserliness in the Runs column did much to consign Australia to such a puny match-losing total. Lastly, he helped his team to turn his debut Test around from a deficit of close to 200 – which wasn't the case with any of those successful debutant bowlers above him on the list.

Above all, this Test marked Vern's arrival like a bright new comet, completing a pace trio with Steyn and Morkel that would play a huge part in South Africa's claiming of the ICC mace a year or so later.

### C. England vs South Africa, Leeds, 2003

*(Has there been a more satisfying photo taken during a South African Test than the one described here?)*

As a daunting prospect for a young player, it couldn't have come much tougher. Monde Zondeki came in to bat on his Test debut at Headingley with South Africa tottering on 142 for seven before a rampant England attack (featuring two pacers named James: 'Curtly' Kirtley and a certain Anderson who would still be playing Tests two decades later). Zondeki was a genuinely fast bowler picked to fill considerable boots: those of the just retired Allan Donald, and temporarily, Shaun Pollock, who was missing this tour through injury. Zondeki was in at No. 9 because his domestic batting record was a little better than the bowlers who followed him, Ntini and Pretorius. Now he was being thrown in at the deepest of deep ends. The one factor in his favour was that his partner was the experienced, gritty opener Gary Kirsten, still there and trying to salvage something from the innings with whatever support he could glean from the tail.

Zondeki must have decided it was just another game, that he had nothing to lose, that fortune favoured the brave, something like that. He began to swing at the England bowlers as if it were a club game, connected a few times, missed several others, and went on swinging until Kirsten came to calm him down with a few words and a pat on the shoulder. He made an entirely unexpected 59 out of a stand of 150, helping Kirsten to his century. Makhaya Ntini, perhaps inspired by the success of his friend from the same rural Border (Eastern Cape) district and cricket-rich school Dale College, also swung lustily to make his top Test score of 32 not out. SA finished on 342, having added exactly 200 for the last three wickets, and were never out of the game after that.

Only 35 behind on first innings, England might have thought they had a sniff when SA were 232 for seven in the second innings. Again the tail came to the rescue. Zondeki, Ntini and Pretorius all gave the talented all-rounder Andrew Hall stout support as he inched toward a maiden Test century, though sadly he was left stranded on 99 not out (Hall would reach the landmark later in an even tougher environment, as a makeshift opener in India). England eventually had a target of over 400 and came nowhere close, with Kallis taking six wickets in one of his irresistible spells that seemed to make specialist bowlers redundant. Zondeki did little with the ball to supplement his brave batting. (Injuries would plague and shorten his four-year Test career.) But his out-of-the-blue half-century in the first innings had already done enough.

And the most pleasant and pleasing Test match photo, my reason for choosing this Test? It shows Gary Kirsten and Monde Zondeki walking off at stumps on the first day after their joint rescue act - arms around each other, both bareheaded, bats tucked under their outside arms. Both men are flushed and glowing with exertion, exhilaration and successful comradeship. An Afrikaans newspaper captioned the photo: *Ai, maar dit was lekker!* "Gosh, that was great!" translates but doesn't capture the breeziness of the original. Nobody in South Africa missed the deeper symbolism. The photo perfectly reflected the best of the New South Africa in cricket. Here was Zondeki (whose uncle was the

ANC struggle activist and later Sports Minister Steve Tshwete), a player selected like Ntini on merit, fitting perfectly into the team and saving it at the hour of need, and here shown in spontaneous camaraderie with a veteran of the old establishment.

The accounts of racial disharmony within the Proteas setup at this time that emerged during a judicial inquiry in the early 2020s – which ended with Graeme Smith and Boucher being cleared of questionable racism charges – failed to tell the whole story. This wonderful photo from the 2003 Headingley Test proved that there was always an opposite dynamic in Proteas teams.

### D. South Africa vs Australia, Johannesburg, 1966

*(I have to abandon the rhetorical questions now, as this choice relates to my home town's summer of reflected glory)*

Cricinfo's Statsguru reacted to a debate among other cricket statisticians in November 2021 about the greatest all-round performances. Feeling that wicket-keeper-batters, a type of all-rounder, were being ignored, Statsguru used the simple methodology of multiplying a batter-keeper's total number of runs by his number of victims, caught and stumped, in a single Test match. The name he came up with, Denis Lindsay of South Africa, is not one remembered often today. I watched a good part of the Test in question, and was glad that Statsguru had caused it to resurface.

Australia were well poised for victory after the first day of the First Test. They'd dismissed the hosts for just under 200, with Lindsay rescuing the innings from complete disaster with 69 from No. 7. The visitors' streetwise if unspectacular opening pair, Simpson and Lawry, looked well set to repeat the double- and triple-century partnerships they'd recorded in England and the West Indies in the last few years. Next day, however, the strong SA pace-seam attack broke the stand and kept the other batters in check, Lindsay catching six of them, but the first-innings deficit was still a significant 126. Graeme Pollock then lit up the Wanderers like an elegant shooting star with 90 in about as many minutes and balls: a typical glorious knock for him, but it was over all too quickly and South Africa needed a longer and bigger innings. Enter 'Lifeboat' Lindsay, as he was already being called. Lindsay made 182 with powerful drives and hooks (some going for six near where I sat). Set almost 500 to win, Australia barely got halfway as Lindsay brought his tally of catches for the match to eight. His runs-wickets product as conceived and highlighted by Statsguru was 2008, a figure exceeding the best achieved by Gilchrist or anybody else.

Lindsay's purple patch lasted all season as he went on to make 606 runs and claim 24 victims in the five-match series. Some of his summer-long glory reflected on his home town of Benoni. The (then) gold-mining town east of Johannesburg had never been remarkable for anything much before; but everyone suddenly knew it as Denis Lindsay's home. Within Benoni, he was feted and lionised as a hero whenever he wasn't away playing cricket; I know because I was living there. People flocked to the downtown sports shop he ran with his father, Johnny Lindsay (also a Test 'keeper) to chat with and be seen with the great man. After that season, Denis never reached quite the same levels and played only two more Tests.

Benoni is known in the cricket world mainly because it was where a more famous Denis, Compton, made 300 in a minute over three hours in 1948, probably the fastest triple century, but the number of balls he faced wasn't recorded. The town, or small city, was barely heard of again until the twenty first century, when it produced two AAA-List celebrities, both blonde beauties with similar names. However, both Princess Charlene of Monaco and 'Princess' Charlize Theron of Hollywood achieved their fame a very long way from their home town. Not so Denis Lindsay. His achievements in the summer of '66/67 gave Benoni a little reflected glory. I hope I wasn't the only ex-Benonian to remember this when a world authority like Cricinfo's Statsguru brought Lindsay's Summer back to cricket's collective memory.

### E. Natal vs Rhodesia: Durban, 1973

(*The choice of this forgotten Currie Cup match has to do with two cricket reasons – definable briefly as 'Richards vs Procter' and 'Jackers' finest hour' – plus one personal reason, which I can best describe as part of the Golden Days of Youth*)

Allow me one match at sub-Test level; you too must have many you remember. I have watched many excellent provincial games in South Africa (where the domestic trophy was known as the Currie Cup for exactly a century up to 1989/90). But this one in Durban stands out - partly because of the mini-battle between two home-town superstars that fronted up the match; partly because of exceptional swing bowling in the opening session by one of the game's real characters; and also because of the sheer joy of watching cricket at Kingsmead at that stage of my life (I was a student and went bodysurfing between sessions, as described in **Bite 39**).

Barry Richards and Mike Procter, born in Durban a year apart, teammates for years, co-stars with complementary skills, were now facing up as rival captains at their home ground of Kingsmead. They'd played together and excelled at SA Schools, provincial, county and Test level. Still the closest of friends, they'd gone separate cricketing ways; Richards was still with Natal and Hampshire, Procter now with Rhodesia and Gloucestershire. Richards was probably the best batter in the world at the time; Procter one of the best fast bowlers. Here they were back at Kingsmead conducting the toss, cricketing Gemini in friendly contention. Yet there were also 20 other players, ready to upstage them.

Procter chose to bowl and began himself to Richards, the perfect start for the fans packing Kingsmead. The titanic mini-clash lasted only three balls, but was utterly memorable. Procter began with three of his trademark express banana-curvers. Richards glided the first one away gracefully behind square for two; came unhurriedly forward to the second; tickled the third for what would have been a four to fine leg with most keepers, but this keeper was an almost 2-metre giant named Gardiner, who managed to sprawl to his left and get a glove under it (Richards' leg glance had been too deliberate to talk of a 'strangle'). The mental video of those three balls is still like an implanted YouTube.

Natal in those days looked vulnerable on the rare occasions that Richards went cheaply at the top, and so it proved now. But to see it as simply as that would have been a grave injustice to Robin Jackman of Surrey and England, Procter's new-ball partner and later a much-loved commentator and raconteur. Whether it was anything to do with the off-shore breeze or the high tide only 500 metres away, both factors often mentioned, Kingsmead could be very conducive to swing bowling at times. I have never seen this advantage utilised better than on this morning by Jackman, as he claimed all of the remaining nine Natal wickets by shortly after lunch to record career-best figures. (Stuart Broad might have been equally unplayable.) I asked 'Jackers' at a function many years later if he would have swopped the other nine for Richards' wicket. He replied, "I'd have got him too if Procky had given me the chance."

Natal, all out for 86, couldn't really hope to come back into the match against the powerful visitors (a stronger team than their successors Zimbabwe have ever had, I believe), but how hard they tried! Batting again the next day some 180 behind, Richards resumed business as usual with an elegant 80-odd, and an allrounder named David Orchard (later a Test umpire) marshalled the tail for his one and only first-class century. Of particular interest was the long tussle in the muggy coastal heat between the Natal batters and three different kinds of quality spin: from Procter, after an initial burst of pace which Richards saw off this time, now bowling his high-calibre off-spinners; Jack du Preez, a leg-spinner who had played Tests for South Africa; and Richie 'Jumbo' Kaschula, a big and ungainly-looking, but highly effective left-arm spinner. (The past and future Test off-spinner Traicos – see **Bite 6** – couldn't even find a place in this side.) Natal in the end had too few to defend, just over 100, but they took five wickets and might have pulled off a heist had they not dropped a catch or two.

Procter had the better of Richards this time (and the points Rhodesia gained helped set up the bizarre events in Bulawayo a few weeks later, as described in **Bite 12**). But after that initial three-ball clash of the home-town superstars, what also makes me remember this game so well is the way that slightly lesser lights like Jackman (especially!) and Orchard outshone their illustrious captains on this occasion. Cricket is a great leveller. And adding to the relish of the match for a starry-eyed young student spectator, was that I managed to watch almost every ball while also fitting in some five or six swims in the surf at Durban's North Beach a few hundred metres away from Kingsmead (see **Bite 39** again if you like).

# K. SUNDRIES

(*Many collections would title this section 'Miscellaneous', a common cop-out word for anything that won't fit neatly into foregoing categories. I have the same dilemma, but prefer to borrow 'sundries', a shorter and much more elegant term, from Australian cricket vocabulary – even if the Aussies themselves no longer use it very often as a synonym for Extras.*)

# 41. ZOMBIE RUBBERS
## (*So-called 'dead rubbers' that are very much alive*)

The World Test Championship has now killed off 'dead rubbers', in the sense that these matches count for points on the WTC log as much as any other Tests. In practice, however, these games have always been anything but 'dead'.

First, however, a word on what seems to have been an interesting evolution of cricket terminology. A 'rubber' in cricket used to mean the same thing as a 'series' of Tests; the term is still used like this in other sports, especially Davis Cup tennis, and even occurs in the cerebral card game Bridge. Therefore any use of 'dead rubber' to describe a single match ought to be wrong. However, my guess is that a 'dead rubber' was originally a series which had already been clinched by one side; and any remaining games were thus 'dead rubber *matches*'. As 'rubber' for a series fell into disuse – it seems to have disappeared in the old cricket sense – I surmise that 'dead rubber match' was shortened to 'dead rubber', with the present-day meaning quite clear.

Such matches are mostly very much 'alive' in the way they are played, in the intensity and competitiveness shown by the teams. The basic motivation is clear enough and goes well beyond the common phrase 'consolation victory'. The side that lost the series is determined to restore some pride and show it is not really inferior, and even that the outcome could have been different with better luck and 'rub of the green'. The series victors, conversely, want to prove that they are deserving winners. However, some dead rubbers have also had a good many other dimensions driving the teams to play as hard as in any 'live' Test.

Two instances involving South Africa featured badly injured batters determined to have their knock for their side, as described at more length in **Bite 43** on 'Crippled Courage' – but in both cases, only the honour of winning or not losing 'dead rubbers' was at stake. A concussed Justin Langer wanted to bat at the Wanderers in 2006 so that Australia could win the series 3-0 instead of 2-1. Graeme Smith exposed his broken hand at Sydney in 2009 in an effort to help his SA side take the series 2-0 instead of 2-1.

Readers in other countries will remember countless such brave efforts. I will add only two historical instances, both of which show how undead 'dead rubbers' have always been, and which also had extra twists. Both showed off that peculiarly British talent for 'doing a Dunkirk': turning a rout into a triumph.

England had to wait for the 15th Ashes Test after World War Two to win a single match against an Australian side that hadn't lost a Test to them or anybody else since 1938. That win was so welcome that E.W. Swanton was moved to bring out both a book and a film titled *Elusive Victory* about the 1951 feat; but the match was as 'dead' as could be, coming with Australia already 4-0 up in the series. It did herald that the worm had turned; England would regain the Ashes two years later.

A famous Test has, as a factual core, an incomplete scorecard that reflects its down-to-the-wire finish. England recovered from 48/5 to chase down 263 with the last pair in. The controlled power hitter Jessop scored 104 in just over an hour (reportedly reaching his century off 76 balls, still an England record as Bairstow's comparable 2022 ton took one ball more); then that last pair, the phlegmatic Yorkshire bowlers Hirst and Rhodes, calmly picked off the 15 runs still needed when they came together. We will probably never know for sure whether Hirst really said to Rhodes at the start of their mission, "We'll get 'em in singles, Wilfred" (they didn't; Rhodes is known to have hit a boundary.) And yet all this happened in a 'dead rubber' after Australia had clinched that 1902 series with a 2-0 lead.

The new WTC dispensation, then, has only confirmed and formalised a reality as old as Test series: that live Test matches never are and never have been 'dead rubbers' as far as the will to win, or the desire to see your team win, is concerned. Test cricket has always been far too vibrant and vital for there to be anything zombie-like about it.

## 42. THE BLOCKATHONS
### (*Cricket's link to the US National Anthem*)

The problem is the remoteness of the two far south-eastern cricket powers. England and South Africa fans have to sacrifice sleep to watch daytime cricket in Australia or New Zealand though Saffers at least don't have to leave bed on a freezing winter morning, as their English counterparts must. In this regard a certain English fan deserves mention. During Ashes Tests Down Under, he would rise at the normal time but then spend his day avoiding all office colleagues, TV's, radios, newspapers or any other source that might tell him the overnight score, so that he could watch the highlights in the English evening, not spoilt by any foreknowledge and hoping for the best. He was generally disappointed on one or both counts: a colleague would spill the beans during the day, and/or England would not be doing very well.

SA or England fans fairly often have the same disincentive to rising early: when their team is under the pump in Australia. If the tourists are going into the last day with several wickets down and no chance of making the required runs to win or avoid an innings defeat, do their supporters really want to get up at five or six A.M. and stumble to the TV, coffee in hand, with the likelihood of being greeted by highlights and a message in the top left corner of the screen saying "Australia won by (an innings and)... runs"?

Yet the fans do and have done that more often than not, hoping against hope to find the match alive, their batters still doggedly "holding the fort". That military analogy, popular for describing defensive batting, strangely occurred to me on an occasion when the batters held the figurative fort. I speak of the drawn Adelaide Test in 2009. One shouldn't compare sport with war, of course (though the common elements, mostly regrettable, are well known). But it was a famous military incident and the globally known song it inspired that came to mind as I watched South African Test debutant Faf du Plessis and five of his partners (of the permissible six) calmly bat out the last day. It had started with SA on four wickets down and few expecting the match to last beyond tea.

The United States national anthem is based on the emotion felt by an American negotiator detained all night on board a British ship off Baltimore during the War of 1812 between the US and its former colonial masters. The American-held Fort McHenry underwent a fierce British bombardment during the night, and the first thing the negotiator, Francis Scott Keyes, wanted to see with the sunrise was whether the US flag was still flying over the fort. It was, and an anthem was born, with its key line "...our flag was still there." Somehow this line came to mind as I tuned in, likewise at sunrise, and saw South African batters still at the crease in Adelaide – though, objective fan that I am, my feeling was less intense than Mr Keyes! The same kind of analogy was applied during South Africa's Anglo-Boer War when the Boers besieging the town of Ladysmith – many of whom knew cricket – sportingly heliographed to the British garrison on the hundredth day of the siege "100 Not Out" and the garrison replied "Ladysmith still batting."

I think it was the Adelaide epic, and especially Faf's role in it, that gave rise to the coining of a new word in cricket's vocabulary – 'Blockathon.' The concept has been around much longer, of course. Every Test team has blocked out a draw at some time or other, sharing the match spoils in one of those endearingly unique features of cricket that distinguish it from other sports. No other sport even has a possible result comparable to a draw.

An analysis of 34 memorable draws in Cricinfo in 2020 identified New Zealand as the most successfully dogged Test team in this regard. England had the most dogged blockathon I remember, and I watched it live. Michael Atherton, more Captain Courageous than Captain Grumpy on this occasion, and keeper Jack Russell stood firm at the Wanderers in 1995 for over four hours to secure a draw. Atherton out-Faffed Faf by opening and batting through the innings, though of course he wasn't making his Test debut. Jack Russell, clenching a figurative bone, was inevitably called 'dogged'. Like SA at Adelaide, England had begun the day on four down and were given very little chance of survival; but unlike SA, they lost only one more wicket all day. English commentators drew parallels with the historic effort by Watson and Bailey that effectively regained the Ashes in the memorable 1953 series.

South Africa have had their share of blockathons. Two efforts beside Adelaide are worth recalling. Oddly, both happened in Sri Lanka, twenty-one years apart, each against a top-flight spinner who was turning the ball sharply without being entirely unplayable.

Jonty Rhodes, best remembered today as one of the great fielders (see **Bite 37D**), could bat a bit too. During South Africa's first full Test tour post-isolation – to SL in 1993 – Rhodes led the resistance against a young Muttiah Muralidharan, later to become the most successful Test bowler of all, as the Proteas hung on eight hours for a draw. Rhodes and a colleague with similar sandy hair and freckled complexion, left-arm spinner (but right-handed bat) Clive Eksteen, played mainly back to Murali's sharp offbreaks for most of the last session to claim a draw that led to a series win.

The scenario was repeated almost exactly in 2014 as several SA batters played well out of character to keep out Rangana Herath's penetrating left-arm spin for just long enough. AB de Villiers made only 12 off 67 balls (underlining how complete a batter he was, able to defend where necessary, as he did alongside du Plessis at Adelaide), while JP Duminy suppressed his natural attacking instincts even more than AB, managing just three off 65 balls. Vernon Philander completed the rearguard action with oddly little visible elation, quietly fending off the last over and tucking his bat under his arm, job done. This blockathon was more significant than the 1993 effort in the greater scheme of ICC things, restoring SA to the No. 1 spot in the Test rankings at the time.

Blockathons are impossible (or pointless) in the white-ball game, of course, but they are part of the magic of traditional cricket. A Cricinfo commentator once wrote that "Test cricket needs a good blockathon every so often." If it involves a major time zone difference, all the more dramatic. Faf's Adelaide epic is unlikely to be the last time that English or Saffer fans rise early to watch a potentially already completed Test in Australia (or super-early for one in New Zealand) and are rewarded by seeing their team's batters still at the crease like the defenders of a beleaguered fort. Americans will forgive a small parody of two lines of 'The Star-Spangled Banner' for such twenty first-century cricket fans who rise at dawn and are glad they did:

*And the smartphone's first Share, and the TV's first glare, Bore proof from afar of our batters still there.*

## 43. CRIPPLED COURAGE
## (*"That's the bravest thing I've ever seen on a cricket field."*)

This was said by someone not given to sentiment or empty praise – it was Ricky Ponting, cast firmly in the mould of the hard-bitten Australian captain as well as being one of the modern great batters. He was speaking to and praising his South African counterpart, Graeme Smith. You'll remember the occasion – Smith had come in to bat at the fall of the ninth SA wicket in the Sydney Test of 2009 with his hand broken and secured by pins, in order to try to help his team gain a draw. The outcome of the series was not even at stake: SA had already clinched their first ever series win in Australia with victories in Perth and Melbourne (although so-called 'dead rubber' matches still carry huge weight in cricket, as seen in **Bite 41**). Smith later described how he'd winced every time his bat met the ball. His ordeal of pain for his side very nearly achieved the desired end: a bare handful of balls remained when Smith was castled by a Mitchell Johnson shooter off a crack that few able-bodied batters could have survived. Ponting walked up to Smith to pay his blunt, powerful compliment as the teams left the field, and the SCG crowd echoed it by rising to Smith.

I don't think anyone pointed out the precedent at the time, but Smith wasn't the first South African captain to bat under such a handicap when his team needed it most. Dudley Nourse made

208 with a fractured thumb, having pain-killing injections at every interval, in the First Test at Edgbaston in 1951; his effort won the match for his side (see **Bite 37A**).

The cynical twenty first-century is not fond of extolling virtues like brave endurance of pain for a cause. But within cricket's unique blend and interaction of individual and team effort, there is still something moving, even stirring, about innings like Smith's and Nourse's where a player suffering a painful and debilitating temporary challenge, just ignores it and 'goes to bat' (literally in this case) for his team. There are many other cameos of this kind; I will recount a few favourites.

Possibly the most heartrending one of all happened in South Africa: the batter at one end was physically hurt and the other one emotionally shattered. It was recalled in 2021, when New Zealand won the first ever World Test Championship, in a Cricinfo piece tracking the evolution of the distinctive Kiwi style of cricket. An earlier NZ team were caught on a Johannesburg pitch at Ellis Park, primarily a rugby ground, which would probably be condemned today as too dangerous for play; soon the fiery SA pacer Neil Adcock had put half the side in hospital. Back home in New Zealand on that Christmas Eve of 1953, the country's worst ever train disaster had claimed 151 lives. The picture of NZ's last wicket pair was unforgettable: at one end, the batter Bert Sutcliffe, one of Adcock's victims, looking like a war casualty with a flapping bandage around his skull; at the other, the bereaved bowler Bob Blair, who had just lost his fiancée in the train tragedy, but had nevertheless marched out to bat amid utter silence from players and spectators. The two, in a kind of metaphor-mixing "make hay in the darkest hour" mood that defied analysis and the SA bowling alike, smashed a quickfire 30 or so.

Many years later I was at a cricket function with John Reid as the guest speaker – not the later J.R. Reid, but the greatest NZ all-rounder before Richard Hadlee. Reid had played in the 1953 match, so I asked what it had all felt like. John Reid hesitated before replying "It was incredibly – emotional" – this from a Kiwi as reluctant to express emotion as Kane Williamson or most of their compatriots of any era. The train tragedy was turned into a TV drama in New Zealand in 2011 called *Tangiwai*, the place where the railway bridge collapsed.

Batters' injuries can all but immobilise them; this sometimes used to bring the now defunct 'runner' into play. One of the most bizarre sights I ever saw on a cricket field, via TV, was when a Natal seam bowler named Rowan Lyle badly damaged a leg during a match and later hobbled in to bat on crutches and with a runner. Whenever he had to take strike, the square-leg umpire solemnly came and took his crutches, Lyle played the ball as best he could, and once he got off strike he was handed his crutches again and limped off to point, where he stood passively while his runner took part in the action. It was like a strange halting ritual, a ballet of gammy grace.

A broken arm in a batter – which some fast bowlers or their captains are said to have told opponents to prepare for – presents other problems. The classic 1963 Lord's Test saw Sir Colin Cowdrey coming in to bat at Lord's with his right arm in a cast, with two balls left, England requiring six runs and West Indies one wicket. Cowdrey was off strike and only had to watch while his partner warded off two thunderbolts from the mighty Windies quick of the time, Wesley Hall. Author Alan Ross wondered how Hall would have bowled if Cowdrey had been on strike. Ross suggested that while the burly quick was bound to try to win the match, he would also have had to remember Cowdrey's condition.

The answer to that perceived moral dilemma came twenty-one years later, when there were no close finishes, just West Indies inflicting an unprecedented 5-0 'blackwash' on England. At Manchester in 1984, the home opener Paul Terry came back with a broken arm to help Allan Lamb complete a century, one of three that the SA-born batter managed in that series off perhaps the greatest Test pace attack ever. Lamb chose to complete this hundred with a brace and expose Terry to an entire over. Joel Garner surgically excised Terry without hurting him further by simply slipping a yorker under his helpless bat – exactly what Hall would most likely have done to Cowdrey.

Concussion is not a condition to be messed about with in cricket or anywhere else, but Justin Langer has had his own experiences of it. Like several New Zealanders half a century before, the opener was felled by a South African bouncer (again in Johannesburg, this time at the New Wanderers Stadium), in his case right at the start of an Australian first innings. Langer suffered concussion and was not expected to take any further part in this 2006 Test. But three days later, two of his bowling teammates, Lee and Kasprowitz, came together with 19 runs required for victory and only the stricken Langer possibly left to bat. ("We'll get 'em this time", the two bowlers probably told each other – as everyone recalled, they had been the pair who just failed to add 60+ for the last wicket in the all-time classic Edgbaston Test a few months earlier). This time they took Australia over the line – but what if they hadn't?

Langer, concussion and all, was determined to bat: he went on record later as saying his captain Ponting told him not to, but Langer recounted "I told Punter if he wouldn't let me bat, he wouldn't be my mate." Whatever Ponting said to Langer, it wasn't anything about the bravest thing on a cricket field, the terms in which he would praise Graeme Smith three seasons later.

Fast forward to 2019, and Langer as Australian coach at the time would preside over the first concussion substitution in Test match history. Again there was a South African connection: the SA-born Marnus Labuschagne became the historic pioneer substitute, replacing the concussed Steve Smith in the cauldron of an Ashes Test at Lord's, no less. Langer must have recalled that day at the Wanderers. One wonders if he agreed with the new rule, wished it had been in force then, or would have done the same again. Whatever the case, Langer is probably still the best of mates with Ponting.

Runners and concussed players continuing on the field now belong only to cricket's past, and that is how it should be. (The runner privilege tended to be controversial, as an England captain, Andrew Strauss, found when he denied South Africa a runner. Strauss then saw a team invitation to a *braaivleis* [barbecue] withdrawn because the Western Cape wine baron hosting the event felt Strauss had acted unsportingly!) But players crippled in one way or another will no doubt continue to display enormous courage at times – the potential for this is woven into the vast canvas of cricket's battles.

## 44. STROKE SUPREMOS
### (*The Handsomest Hooker alongside two greats*)

The unnamed guest speaker, for reasons too involved to recount here, was sozzled, legless, blind drunk, rat-arsed (whichever expression you prefer) by the time he stood up to address the cricket function. He managed to get out only seven words before he keeled over, but they were deeply significant: "Wally Hammond was a jolly good player." The writer who relates this anecdote (whose name I admit to having forgotten) added: "A single vision must have emerged from the mists of alcohol, *possibly a perfectly executed cover drive* [my italics]. There can have been no greater compliment to a cricketer."

Hammond's cover drive, by all accounts (and some surviving footage), was a thing of beauty that deserved to be so celebrated. South Africans saw their fair share of it when he captained England on the last pre-war tour here, especially during the concluding 'Timeless Test', in which he was the last batter to be dismissed. As late as the 1990s, the opener Roy Pienaar – whose off-side driving had a flourish derived mainly from a high follow-through – could still be introduced as "South Africa's own Wally Hammond" (this at a function where I can vouch that the presenter was entirely sober).

A typical stroke by an even greater batter than Hammond was described by the doyen of cricket writers, Sir Neville Cardus, like this: "Bradman's best shot was off the back foot; neither cut nor drive but something in between, it raced to the boundary faster than any other stroke by any other man". Others wrote that this type of Bradman shot went like a tracer bullet to the fence, or similar comparisons. So we have two kinds of stroke deeply linked in cricket's collective memory with two of its megastars. I am going to add a third player who doesn't appear to belong on anywhere near the same page as that august pair. This may astonish you and perhaps make you question my own sobriety. I can only reply that this section is about the stroke as much as the player and that these are personal impressions, based on cricket I have watched myself as well as read about.

I'm not saying for one moment that Kevin McKenzie of Transvaal (now Johannesburg's Lions franchise) was anywhere near in the league of Bradman or Hammond (very few batters have been), but he was very good indeed. Ask anyone who watched him play provincially for over a decade and for 'South Africa' against various rebel touring teams in the 70s and 80s (his son Neil would have a Test career). McKenzie was generally described as 'stylish' or 'the Transvaal stylist': his drives had a sort of graceful flowing quality, the back foot somehow following the front one as he 'walked' into the shot. A hook seems too violent a stroke to be associated with grace or style; but McKenzie's hook had a kind of panache that was almost graceful: for me, he was the 'Handsomest Hooker'.

(A word of explanation here of my tongue-in-cheek subtitle for this section. I mean of course that McKenzie's hooking was more handsome than that of other batters. I avoided calling him 'The Happy Hooker', even though this was a very popular nickname for some sportsmen at the time. It was applied to batters who liked hooking and to rugby hookers [players in a key position among a team's forwards]. The joking reference was to the title of the then best-selling autobiography of a famous career call girl.)

McKenzie was fearless in hooking bouncers headed for his cap badge; he played in the era when helmets were just coming in, but never wore one that I saw. He was also fearless about deep fielders set in a trap to catch him; he simply took them on, clearing them or beating them much more often than he holed out. To illustrate this, I will describe one particular over of remarkable McKenzie hooking that I watched at the Wanderers. The bowler was one of the fastest, Sylvester Clarke of Barbados. Clarke would have played for West Indies far more often had they not had so many outstanding pacers then, and this was why he was in South Africa with one of the Windies rebel teams.

Clarke knew about McKenzie's hooking and there were men out at deep square leg and fine leg. There were no real restrictions on the number of bouncers at the time. It was only a question of how many he would bowl in succession. A mini-epic followed. The first bouncer was hooked to perfection, bisecting those two fielders as it crossed the boundary on a single hop. Ditto the second, except I think there were two hops. Clarke directed his third bouncer outside the off stump; McKenzie hooked again, and top-edged over the keeper. Clarke bounced one more, even further outside the off; this time McKenzie's hook flew high over first slip. Four boundaries: the first two from hook strokes that were perfection, the other two, cases of fortune favouring the bold. Clarke did not bowl another bouncer to McKenzie that day.

Sir Vivian Richards was said to be a brilliant hooker, and from what I have seen of him on YouTube he might stand out as the all-time international exponent of the shot (I open myself to considerable challenge on this one). He too batted before helmets; and he had to face Lillee and Thomson at their height. Earlier, Australia's Stan McCabe thrillingly took on Larwood's Body-line bouncers with hooks or pulls: the ball was said to have crashed into the railings before McCabe's left foot came back to the ground. But I will stick with McKenzie when it comes to the hook, based in part on that one over I watched at the Wanderers.

Hammond's cover drive; Bradman's back-foot drive/cut/chop; Kevin McKenzie's hook. What counterparts are there today? In honesty I find it difficult to associate any current batter with any particular stroke. The amount of short-format cricket and modern field placings require even ordinary batters to be able to hit at least adequately to almost any corner of the field, with shots orthodox and unorthodox.

You will have your own preferences, which I will try to guess at. You may of course picture Kieron Pollard blasting ball after ball into the upper tiers behind the sightscreen; but many batters today do that, and I am not thinking of that kind of shot. You may think of Joe Root placing a cover drive exquisitely out of reach of the infield and timed well enough to beat the sweeper. You may imagine Kane Williamson threading a late cut (or 'back cut') with pinpoint precision between gully and point, with just enough on it to beat the third man to the rope. Strokes by Babar Azam or Virat Kohli may come to mind (Kohli's logic-defying loft over long-off from the *back* foot against Pakistan in the 2022 T20 World Cup must go down as one of the single most unforgettable shots). Steve Smith's generally awkward technique makes it hard to single out any particular stroke, but his pull in front of square is the closes he gets to good-looking.

It was once said of a batter regarded as unorthodox in his time, "If he ever read the coaching manual, he must have been holding it upside down." Since the range of common cricket strokes began expanding a few decades ago to include the reverse sweep, scoop, ramp switch hit and other innovations, the manual has probably gone online and become three-dimensional. I won't try to single out any player who executes any of these newer shots more memorably than others. Kevin Pietersen will of course be remembered for inventing the switch hit as well as his 'flamingo shot', with the back leg high in the air, which must have caused keepers and close fielders to salivate at the untenanted crease – if KP had given them any chance to secure the ball in time to break the stumps.

There is probably a vision of one modern batter playing one kind of shot lurking somewhere in your subconscious. Bring it to the surface by all means – but perhaps not by drinking as much as that guest speaker who gave Hammond's cover drive the ultimate accolade.

## 45. 'YOU GOT TO SHOW SOME RESPECT'
## ("*I don't like cricket. Oh no! I love it*" – *10cc*)

10cc's hit song *Dreadlock Holiday* is not just a ditty about a tourist experiencing the seamier side of Kingston life; it also contains a good deal of insight into the Jamaican and wider Caribbean outlook. Respect is very important, as the line I've borrowed for this Bite's title shows. Later in the song, one mugger even shows a little respect for the victim by offering him one dollar for his silver chain, and the tourist gets off relatively lightly by showing respect and love for Jamaica and its local pastimes of cricket and reggae. Even the line "Don't you queer me pitch" could refer to the revered turf of Sabina Park.

The insistence on respect in the West Indies, especially in the light of the islands' history, has been closely tied to cricket. The ground-breaking 2010 documentary *Fire in Babylon* and much of the writings of Tony Cozier trace how cricket was the chief means by which West Indians were able to outdo their former colonial masters and earn their respect. Former England captain Tony Greig made the worst possible mistake when, after being named to lead a tour to the Caribbean, he promised to make the opposition 'grovel.' His South African roots didn't help the situation. It was Greig and England that grovelled. He later found an easier target for his disrespect in the world cricket establishment, acting as chief recruiter and facilitator for the Packer Revolution.

The chief hatchet-men and enforcers of cricket's role in that quest for respect, the long litany of Windies quicks in the 1970s and 80s, also expected it on a personal level. Sir Curtly Ambrose once sent a British correspondent packing for requesting an interview with him through a team-mate. The Brit reporter was told he should have come to ask Curtly himself. He plucked up his courage and did so, but the answer was predictably a curt(ly) No.

Fast bowlers of other countries have also demanded respect. During one World Cup, Allan Donald found a batter coming out to face him in a sunhat – cricket's equivalent of a red rag to a bull. Sultan Zarawani of the United Arab Emirates couldn't bat, bowl or field very well, but the UAE wanted an Emirati to captain their team of Asian expatriates, essentially reducing their XI to a X. Donald, clearly seeing the lack of a helmet as a sign of disrespect, told his team-mates he was going to 'ping' the batter. Captain Hansie Cronje should probably have intervened at that point. Donald duly poleaxed Sultan with a pinpoint bouncer to the forehead beneath the sunhat and put him in hospital (after the batter had faced a further six balls still without a helmet, showing bravado in line with his privileged position, even if he wasn't a real Sultan). The consequences could have been like Larwood's hits in the Body-line series, or worse; Donald says in his autobiography that he feared he'd killed Zarawani. 'White Lightning' probably handled perceived disrespect better for the rest of his career.

An earlier pacer had little respect for persons or for the English class system, at least if even some of the stories told about Fred Trueman – who attracted tall tales as a stereotype of the blunt, plainly spoken fast bowler – are true. In one such story, a posh-looking batter came in to face him and took a peculiar stance: his front foot was cocked upwards with only the toes on the ground. Trueman asked the non-striker who this batter was and why he stood like that. "That's Lord Proudfoot, and he always stands like that." "Right," said Fred in broad Yorkshire, "he won't to me." The next ball, a pinpoint fast yorker onto the offending cocked foot, left Lord Proudfoot hopping about in pain and hobbling for some days. Clearly Trueman, a 'working class hero' as well as a feared pacer, felt disrespected as much by the implication of class distinction as by the strange stance. (Note: I admit to inventing the lord's name; the rest of the story is attributed to Trueman himself in the unremembered book where I read it.)

Genuine fast bowlers, quicks, pacers, whatever you call them, are a breed apart, and don't come along that often. They add immense value; the game needs more than there are around in 2022. Will the Caribbean conveyor belt produce more pacers with that look of smouldering aggression, of brooding menace, which marked all the *Fire in Babylon* hitmen? The current crop of Windies quicks seem too nice for that – take your friendly Alzarri and Kemar, your ever-smiling Jason and your young Jayden. But this is still a space to watch.

New hostile fast bowlers will emerge, whether in the Caribbean or elsewhere. They will deserve respect as much as their predecessors. The enforcement of that respect may or may not be as drastic as in the past. In the meantime, it would be wise just to 'show some respect', whether you are in Kingston or anywhere else. And do wear a helmet if you ever have to bat against one of them.

## 46. REST OF THE WORLD XI's – SOME TRIUMPHS AND A FLOP
### *(Including the 'best' match I have watched)*

The flop was the most recent and turned out to be a waste of effort and resources, so we are not likely to see any Rest of the World XI's again. But the two triumphs are very good memories. We have all played the fun game of picking a World XI from current players; but until there is inter-galactic travel to another inhabited and cricket-playing world, such a team will have no real opponent. Rest of the World, or ROW, XI's are a bit more viable. Let's look at the four such teams that have played serious matches – and whole series in three cases – and try to judge if the concept has any value.

### a. ROW XI 2005/6: The Flop

The trouble with this ROW team was really that Australia's 'Indomitables' (as Brett Lee dubbed the side he played in, echoing the 1948 'Invincibles') had suffered the worst possible blow to their pride. Australia had just lost the Ashes, against all expectations, to a determined England team playing at home. They were soon granted a sop to their injured pride with a series against a ROW XI, implying that they were still the best team in the world. But they still had a massive point to prove, which they could best do by obliterating the ROW. This they did with ruthless efficiency over one 'Test' and three 'ODI's. Graeme

Smith captained the multinational side and, with the likes of Gayle, Sangakkara, Flintoff, Pietersen and Muralidharan (Smith was especially thrilled to have a world-class spinner at his disposal), really seemed to think they had a chance. But the problem was probably motivation. A Cricinfo commentator put his finger on it when he wrote of a Flintoff-Pietersen partnership for the ROW in one of the 'ODI's: "They were never likely to repeat their Ashes heroics in such an artificial cause." An artificial cause it then seemed indeed; the whole disastrous exercise underlined that players, consciously or not, need to be playing for their nation to give of their best in international matches.

### b. ROW XI 1987: A match to remember

There are ways to overcome the problem of patriotic motivation, however; and this game found them. First, let both teams be multinational, so you don't have a proud national team set against a motley crew. Second, make the match a huge celebration of cricket, something players are proud and feel privileged to take part in. This can only happen on rare, generally one-off occasions.

The 1987 match was one such, a kind of unprecedented cricket fiesta. The MCC, Marylebone Cricket Club, had existed since 1787. To celebrate its bicentenary, the storied club decided to hold a cricket extravaganza. The best players in the world, forming two well matched sides, were needed to ensure a contest worthy of the occasion. The club came up with an excellent formula to achieve this. All those who played for English counties (who, then as now, included many but not all of the best overseas players) would play as a composite team under the MCC banner; and their opponents would be chosen from the remainder of the best players everywhere, to be called the Rest of the World XI. It all worked like a charm.

This became personal. When I read about the match, I decided to watch it, even if it meant taking long leave from my Johannesburg-based work so that I could include it in a trip around the UK, a country which I had read reams about, but never then visited. As a South African cricket tragic, I had more motivation than most. I had never watched (live) all the stars then playing Test cricket, because SA had been isolated from the international game since 1970. Now here was the chance to see all, or most, of them together in one glorious game. The match would be worth all the effort and expense of getting there. And so it proved.

You can read all the details of the game online or, if you have it, the Wisden Cricket Anthology, where it's the selected extract for 1987. Everything, for me, came up to expectations. Being at Lord's, the 'home of cricket', and looking at such familiar landmarks as the Father Time weathervane in real life, was a thrill in itself. The sun shone gloriously, for four days at least. Gooch, Gavaskar, Gatting and Greenidge all scored centuries, a kind of G-force harnessed in the service of cricket itself, against the finest bowlers. Even ostracised South Africa was represented by Clive Rice, playing for the MCC in his capacity as Notts captain – which didn't deter Saffers in the crowd, myself included, from cheering in Afrikaans when he walked out to bat. His fellow great all-rounders of the 80s, Richard Hadlee, Imran Khan and Kapil Dev (though not Botham) were also playing. Gooch was run out by possibly the best bit of fielding by a bowler ever seen (see **Bite 1**). I had never watched such cricket.

It didn't even matter that the last day was washed out with the match well poised. Such a game would almost have been spoiled by one side winning. Besides, I'd wanted to experience cricket in its ancestral heartland of England; and a day being lost to rain was certainly very much part of that tradition.

Was MCC vs the ROW XI the 'best' match I've ever attended? If 'best' refers to the accumulated quality of the players on show, I would say it was. Obviously many Tests have come close to the teams in terms of overall playing skills and have surpassed the match in terms of competitiveness, excitement and tension. Still, everybody agreed that it had been superb match and altogether worth playing. So as far as the record of Rest of the World XI's is concerned, this was a clear triumph.

### c. ROW XI 1970 and 1971/2: two excellent 'Test' series

It was the strength of the England and South Africa Test teams at the time that brought this series and pioneering concept about, I believe. The planned SA tour of England in 1970 had been billed as a showdown to determine the No. 1 team in the world. South Africa had just defeated Australia 4-0; England had beaten the West Indies away and at home in the last two years and tied the last Ashes series; and India and Pakistan were not yet the forces they would become. But then the tour was cancelled and England had to fill the hole – an English non-war summer with no touring team has been unthinkable for decades. But no team of the strength of South Africa was available for the expected showdown. So somebody had the idea of replacing them with an even stronger side, a Rest of the World team. The South African players that the English public most wanted to see could still be invited, and were.

And it all worked out perfectly. The ROW XI carried too many guns and won 4-1, but England were always competitive. The English crowds were enthralled to watch the array of international stars – not least the South Africans Barry Richards, Graeme and Peter Pollock, Mike Procter and Eddie Barlow. A glorious partnership between Graeme Pollock and Gary Sobers, impossible in any other context, went down in cricket folklore (see **Bite 46**) .Even South African fans, disappointed but not too surprised by the cancellation, felt almost compensated by such an excellent series featuring several of their players in prominent roles. The SABC carried regular radio commentary (no TV in SA then), which most Saffer fans followed – including a cricket-mad fourteen-year-old schoolboy.

A Rest of the World XI replaced a scheduled South African tour for the second and last time on a tour to Australia in 1971/2. A slightly weaker ROW XI than the one in England the previous year took on an Australian team in transition. But that transition saw two emerging stars give notice of the heights that they would reach in the next decade. A new young fast bowler named Dennis Lillee took a staggering 8/25 in one of the matches, while a new Chappell, Greg, showed that his established brother Ian wasn't the only one in the family who could 'bat a bit'. On the World side, Sobers scored a 254 that many rated as his greatest innings ever, and Pollock a century, though this time round there wasn't another partnership of the peerless left-handers. The ROW XI edged a hard fought four-game series 2-1 that was never given Test match billing, but would have justified the status in terms of playing quality and competitiveness.

**d. Summary and future, if any, of ROW XI's**

The question arises in retrospect: why did the ROW players perform so well in 1970 and '71/72, but so poorly in 2005? Player motivation is a tricky issue, but I think it had to do with the perceived status of the 1970 contest: these matches 'felt' like a genuine Test series to players and fans alike – and were initially recognised as such. The 1971/2 series wasn't far behind. By contrast, the one-off multi-day match played by Smith's ROW in

2005 had nothing remotely comparable in feel, perception or status. The ICC did later annul the Test status of the 1970 series (much to the relief of the statisticians, who'd always had to add awkward footnotes to the Test records of the players involved); but that doesn't detract from the high calibre and resounding success of the first ROW initiatives. Strangely, the 2005 flop is listed in some Test records.

So the score from past 'experiments' is 2-1 in favour of the ROW concept (or 3-1 if you take the two series played between 1970 and '72 separately). Are we likely to see another one? Certainly the firmer entrenchment of a No. 1 Test nation with the new World Test Championship will always provide a team for the ROW to play against. But there is a danger that the 2005 motivation shortfall might be repeated, and even a single Test (or 'Super-Test') involving players from several countries would have to be squeezed into an over-full calendar these days.

However, another all-star fiesta game like the one in 1987 is a most attractive idea. 2027 will be the 150$^{th}$ anniversary of the first Test match, if you need an occasion to celebrate. The Rest of the World XI concept need not be binding. You could look at something like the Northern against the Southern Hemisphere ('dibs' on any Kenyan, Singaporean or other equatorial players could be negotiated); or maybe Asia vs the Rest. The idea of a multinational team, or of two such teams playing each other, still has its appeal. I hope we see such games again.

# 47. TIMELESS TESTS – PAST THEIR TIME?
## (*Will – or should – there ever be another one?*)

It was two matches, not just one as is often thought, that gave Timeless Tests a bad name. We know about the eleven-day marathon in Durban in March 1939 with its farcical ending that is usually given the TT label. But if by 'Timeless' you mean a match played to a finish, the 1938 Oval Test a few months earlier, had also sat badly in some ways. The young prodigy Hutton making a record 364 was fine, but the talk that England should have pushed on to the 1000 mark just because they could, was less fortunate. Bradman fell out of the match, injured while having a rare bowl, so Australia's chances of achieving any parity once England passed 700 or so were slim. I think it was only some kind of sense of proportion, perhaps related to 'the spirit of cricket', that caused the England captain Hammond to relent and declare on 903-7 with a top batter (Hardstaff) still there and in full cry (I can't imagine Hammond ever taking pity on any Australian team). Australia lost by an innings and almost 600, still a Test record. I believe it was a general sense of excess and disproportion about this match that began the demise of play-to-a finish matches, even before the Durban endurance event the following year.

I have a few personal insights into what we erroneously call

'The Timeless Test', as my father was at high school in Durban then and passed them on to me. He said the match took on a hypnotic fascination, like a long-running serial, and that many people, some not even cricket fans, looked in on Kingsmead regularly to take in the atmosphere of the seemingly endless match. One employer who'd promised his staff time off to watch 'the whole Test' (Tests in SA were much rarer then), reneged and recalled them to work after a week. When the end finally came, it became known that the SA captain Melville had wanted to claim the match, arguing that it was the England team who were walking away to catch their train and then ship. Durban bookies had to fob off punters who'd bet on a home victory and wanted their money on the same argument as Melville!

(Something very similar had happened at Bridgetown, Barbados in 1930, in the sense that West Indies and England were playing a dragged-out 'Timeless Test', but this MCC party's voyage home also wouldn't wait and a draw was agreed. This match carries far less aura than the Durban one, perhaps because of the respective fourth-innings scores when time was called on the supposedly timeless contests. England at Kingsmead were on 654-5, just 42 short of completing a 696 chase that would surely have remained the record forever, whereas Windies on 408-5 at Kensington Oval were less than halfway to a notional 836.)

Six long war years gave cricket people plenty of time to reflect on the Durban and (London) Oval Tests; it was decided they'd been bad for cricket, and when Tests resumed, all play-to-a-finish matches were dropped. Tests played that way in Australia in the 1920s and 30s had in fact never extended beyond the seventh day at the most (kudos to all the toiling bowlers who'd somehow found ways to winkle good batters out on mainly flat pitches). But a real 'Timeless Test' (nine playing days in Durban, eight in Bridgetown, with no play on the Sundays) had always been waiting to happen.

TV scheduling and the whole rushed ethos of the twenty first century would be entirely against the principle. Nevertheless, there were those who called for the inaugural WTC final in 2021 and all its successors to be played to a finish, if only to determine a winner from the match and not the league standings. It won't happen for these finals or any other match. Cricket is too fond of the draw as one of the possible long-format outcomes, a feature unique among all sports. Nobody will again crack jokes like "*The English, not being a very religious people, invented cricket to give themselves an idea of eternity*", or write, as someone did in the timeless test era, "*England had to make 617 to win, with all eternity in which to get them.*"

Such notions are not appropriate to Test cricket, if they ever were. The 'blockathon' is still a unique and valued part of the five-day format, as seen in **Bite 42**. But it needs the goal of a draw to keep the batters grimly holding the fort. You can't deadbat until the stars begin to fall.

## 48. IF YOU COULD TIME TRAVEL…
## (*Which Test or series in the past would you watch?*)

This type of fun exercise in science fiction fantasy always comes with a serious existential question. If you could go back, for example, to 1933 and assassinate the newly empowered Adolf Hitler, the whole historical applecart would be upset (and cricket would have had its potentially fascinating 1940/1 and 1942 Ashes series, for one thing). So let's say you are a sort of disembodied spirit present at an earlier time, able to see and hear anything, but invisible, inaudible, unable to touch or be touched, and therefore powerless to change any of the events that happened. And as an arbitrary cut-off date for cricket events, we will take 1955, before which most of us could not have personally experienced any Tests or series.

My choice, and perhaps yours, would fall in Hitler time: the Body-line series of 1932/3 and specifically the Third Test, the 'Adelaide Earthquake' as David Frith called it in his penetrating *Bodyline Autopsy*. It was the human drama; the shock waves rippling far beyond cricket; the shaking to the foundations of all the assumptions about sportsmanship and non-sportsmanship contained in the then still common saying 'It's not cricket'.

Imagine it. You are there at the Adelaide Oval, perhaps even on the field as you are disembodied. You want to run with the

England fielders and the Australian non-striker to assist Woodfull when he is hit by Larwood and totters to the ground; then the same for Oldfield. Or you are in the crowd hearing them howl in protest. You don't approve of the verbal abuse and physical missiles that they hurl at the blameless England boundary fielders. But perhaps you have more sympathy with them when Jardine comes to patrol the boundary himself and contemptuously turns his back on the barrackers.

You can see those "great leaping long hops", as on-the-spot writer Denzil Batchelor described Larwood's bouncers, for yourself. You can judge at first hand whether Bradman was fast-footed enough to have backed away from the short-pitched expresses and slashed them away into the empty off-side spaces, avoiding Jardine's leg-trap of six or seven men. (A later writer on the series, Ronald Mason, suggested that Bradman could have countered Body-line this way, but chose not to, because he sensed correctly that it would be a one-season phenomenon and soon outlawed.)

Being disembodied and invisible, you can pass through closed doors and eavesdrop on the key private conversations of this turbulent tour. You can see the expression on Sir Pelham Warner's face when the England manager goes to the Australian dressing room to see how Woodfull is, and is told by the prostrate and stricken Australian captain that only one side out there is playing cricket. Better still, you can listen in earlier when Allen, alone among Jardine's four fast bowlers, tells the captain and architect of Body-line that he will not bowl the way Jardine wants. You can hear the exact words that Allen uses in his refusal, being Jardine's social equal – amateur, elite school – unlike Larwood and the other two professional pacers, whose jobs could have been on the, well, Body-line.

You can even watch the almost comic scene in a Brisbane hospital ward when two England players 'snatch' a team-mate admitted with tonsillitis while playing in the Fourth Test to go and bat, over the protests of the ward sister. The stricken specialist batter, Eddie Paynter, handled this abrupt plunge into the action and torrid heat so well that he scored 83, which proved crucial in clinching the series – and then returned to hospital to continue his treatment. You may hear what the doctor doing ward rounds said to Paynter that evening. You can be back at the ground a few days later to see the recovered Paynter win the match and series with a six.

Returning now to the real world and personal experiences, two answers I have heard from guest speakers at cricket functions in South Africa cast a good deal of extra light on Body-line many decades after the event. Eric Rowan, the long-serving and distinguished SA opener, was asked who had been the fastest bowler ever he'd faced. Without hesitating, he replied "Larwood. When I faced him at Trent Bridge, I didn't see his first three balls." Rowan was referring not to any Test, but to the tour match against Notts in 1935, more than two years after the Body-line series brought about Larwood's effective expulsion from Test cricket. For perspective, Rowan would later open in Tests against the legendary Australian pace duo of Lindwall and Miller in 1949/50, when he was one of the very few SA batters who could cope with them.

Chris Harte, a visiting Australian cricket historian, was asked at a SA Cricket Society meeting, "Is it true that Douglas Jardine is still the most hated man in Australia?" His reply was indirect but interesting. "I had some long interviews with Bradman about Body-line. He would never name Jardine, but always referred to him as 'the English captain'. So yes, it goes pretty deep." This chimed with the incident during Bradman's last tour in 1948, when Jardine, long retired and perhaps more mellow by then, invited some of the younger Australian tourists for a drink. Bradman flatly refused them permission to go.

The 'Adelaide Earthquake' and the Body-line series, then, would be my choices. If my time traveller's licence were extended to one more Test, I might go and watch that crazy match in Barbados in 1935, when the pitch was so bad that the West Indies and England captains had to gamble on how many runs to put on the board in each innings while reversing their batting orders and declaring on very low scores to get the other in. (Times change: Kohli and Root didn't follow this example during the two-day test on a possibly even worse pitch at Ahmedabad in 2020, allowing Root as a part-time off-spinner to get an unlikely five-for.)

For a series, the Australia-West Indies contest of 1960/1 that began with the first Tied Test would be a very strong candidate. But I would choose 1952/3, when a SA touring team that some people said was so weak that the tour should be cancelled, tied a series with the mighty Australia. This choice is not based on Saffer patriotism, but the fact that I was so exposed to so many verbal and written references to the tour while growing up. (These included the first Afrikaans book I read by choice, *Amper Wêreldkrieketkampioene* – Almost Cricket World Champions. The title was debatable, but the book was certainly the first about cricket to be written in that language.)

Even with an unlimited Time Travel pass, it should be added in fairness, the most avid cricket-historical buff of today would find it hard to fix on any series at any time that, objectively viewed, could equal or surpass a series played well within contemporary experience – the 2005 Ashes.

Cricket has always had a special relationship with time. There is the umpire's call at stumps; the Father Time weathervane at Lord's; the Timeless Tests that weren't; the newest mode of dismissal, Timed Out. If science can master time exploration as it has space exploration, it would only be fitting for cricket aficionados to be among the first to go time travelling. Which Test or series would you choose?

## 49. AB AND SHERLOCK HOLMES: A CRI-FI FANTASY
### *(If you don't like fantasy or non-cricket allusions, skip the whole bit in italics.)*

Abraham Balthasar de Villiers (no wonder he was always known as AB) did not earn the nickname 'Mr 360' for nothing. To get the ball to any unpatrolled corner of the field, he would "play every shot in the book and a few besides" (this could also have been said of Denis Compton, who apparently played innovative shots that nobody had a name for in his day – Compton could no doubt have played T20 cricket with little adjustment). As promised, I will highlight AB's special ability with a short piece of light-hearted fictional fantasy:

*Sir Arthur Conan Doyle was turning his talents to a cricket story, as Sherlock Holmes was away rescuing his younger sister Enola from the clutches of his arch-rival Moriarty. Doyle explained his idea to friends: England, busy being thrashed by Australia in a home Ashes series, had discovered an unknown bowler named Tom Spedegue who had perfected the 'dropper'. This was a treetop-high vertical full toss that dropped, also almost vertically, with pinpoint accuracy onto the stumps. With its novelty and shock value, the 'dropper' baffled the Australian batters and they were initially routed. However, they soon mastered the new delivery with what Doyle called the 'back* drive'.

"Back drive, Arthur?" a fellow MCC member asked Doyle. "What kind of shot is that and how do you play it? Isn't the batsman facing the wrong way?" "Good point. I know how to deal with that. There's a batsman who can play shots to every possible corner of the field, so much so they call him Mr 360. I shall enlist his services to show that a back drive is feasible." "Balderdash, Arthur, nobody bats like that. Tell you what, we'll make it a wager. Place a bottle on the boundary at long-stop, directly behind the stumps. Then let a bowler toss up this very high donkey drop – sorry, you call it a 'dropper' – falling straight onto the stumps, and let your batsman try to drive it backwards so he breaks the bottle. Fifty quid says he can't. Even Jessop couldn't do it. Who's this wonderful batsman of yours anyway?" "Don't worry about that. You won't recognise him anyway when you see him." Conan Doyle didn't want to divulge anything about the Time Machine recently created by an inventor and fellow writer he knew, H.G. Wells. The invention was still being kept very much under wraps in case the military, currently engaged in a major war in South Africa, should get hold of it. But Wells, who'd been using his Time Machine to watch cricket in the future, had told him about Mr 360, and Doyle was confident that this gifted batter could be teleported backwards through time to win his bet.

A.B. de Villiers couldn't remember much about his journey to London, but that was not unusual with the amount of travelling he did. He was more alarmed by the newspaper headlines about a war in South Africa, but his mobile phone didn't seem to be working and he couldn't find out more. Other things seemed peculiar too, like the clothes people wore and the use of horse-drawn vehicles with very few cars. Despite these concerns, he did his best to reply politely to the strange cricket questions that this well-spoken English gentleman was asking him.

"Look, Mr Doyle, I might be able to hit your bottle by playing a scoop or a ramp –" "A what?" Doyle assumed these odd words were part of professional cricketers' jargon. "Ramp, scoop, you know, like this or this...(AB demonstrated) Or I could turn towards the keeper as the ball drops, switch to a tennis grip and play an overhead long forearm; that way I'd give myself the best chance of hitting your bottle. I used to play tennis, you know, as well as squash, rugby, golf –" "All right, that's enough -" Doyle interrupted, dropping his ashtray in irritation, which AB caught reflexively, "- you sound like Charles Fry. No, don't play any of your scamps and scraps and Roopes – they don't look anything like a drive. And you can't come to Lord's and play tennis; it just wouldn't be cricket. Can't you just turn and face the stumper, as you say, and play a back drive as I described, just as you would a normal forward drive to a full toss?" "It might be tricky to a ball like this 'dropper' of yours, Mr Doyle. If you try to drive a high full toss, it's easy to be caught and bowled. Or in this case, caught by the keeper. But I'll tell you what –"

Just then Sherlock Holmes walked in with his sister Enola, whom he'd successfully rescued from Moriarty. The problem was explained to him. Holmes knew little about cricket, but with his speed-reading skill he quickly went through a copy of the Laws of the game in five minutes. Two minutes later the great detective had a solution.

"Elementary, gentlemen. You need merely have a pipe of appropriate length placed with one end just above the wicket at which Mr Villiers is batting and the other above the bottle on the boundary which is the objective. The pipe should be open at both ends. Nothing in the Laws of Cricket forbids this and the hindrance to the wicket-keeper is of no account. Mr Villiers, as I approached, I observed the speed and dexterity with which you caught Mr Doyle's ashtray a few minutes ago. I deduce that you are gifted with outstanding reflexes and co-ordination. You will therefore have no difficulty in striking a ball delivered in the manner envisaged, as it drops towards your stumps, precisely into the opening of the pipe above the wicket. The ball will then run through the pipe and shatter the bottle at the other end, thereby winning your bet, Mr Doyle."

Enola Holmes, a brilliant and feisty girl, was listening attentively. Her boyfriend played cricket and she knew her brother's plan would be laughed at. But she immediately saw how the idea could be adapted for a new version of another popular sport.

Many decades later, Enola's grandchildren found her notes in an attic. They loved the concept and set about putting it into practice, eventually on a world-wide scale. That is how the golf spinoffs of Putt-Putt and Miniature Golf were born.

AB de Villiers, who loves all sport, once tried a round of Putt-Putt. He was annoyed with himself for missing one putt on the 18 par-two holes and therefore carding only a 19. He had no inkling of his presence at the moment that the game was first conceived.

The Time Machine (destroyed in the far distant future before it could become widely known or used) had included a MEME, or Memory Erasure Mechanism Extraordinary. Despite this, AB felt a prickly sense of eerie recognition when, browsing in a Bengaluru bookshop between IPL games near the end of his career, he happened to pick up a short story about cricket by the

*Sherlock Holmes author. It had someone playing a 'back drive' to a 'dropper'. And he could never explain how he had once found five old English ten-pound notes in his wallet.*

(On a more serious note for those interested in the possibility of a 'back drive', I have read of a stroke being described as such, played at Lord's in 1928. The first great West Indian all-rounder, Sir Learie Constantine, facing the English off-spinner Vallance Jupp, turned around and 'drove' the ball over an apprehensive wicket-keeper to the sightscreen. This description came from the leading radio commentator of the time, Howard Marshall, who actually used the verb 'drive', according to the writer Peter West in his memories of Marshall. Today, T20 batting produces such gyrations and pirouettes by batters that a stroke something like this would not be at all surprising in the format. I think I do remember a Cricinfo commentator describing a shot in a T20 game as a 'back drive' without going into more detail, which was a pity. But finding footage of Constantine's shot in some archive would be the first prize in the quest for Conan Doyle's mythical back drive.)

# L. DRAWING STUMPS

## 50. FORMATS AND THE FUTURE
### (*Out of the mouth of babes*)

Conversing with an eight-year-old is easy and fun if you have a common topic about which you are both passionate; and what better such than cricket? In 2020, a friend's grandson was playing for his school's Under-10 team, in a mini-league on Saturday mornings, and on the lawns of our townhouse complex every free moment even in the southern winter, if any other boy would forsake the oval ball to join him. I asked him, "Who's your favourite player?" and wasn't surprised at the reply, "Quinton." Every South African fan of teenage years or younger adores the dashing batter-keeper, not just for his play but his eternally youthful look. ('QdK' had to grow a moustache to stop writers and commentators from calling him a 'wunderkind', 'a startled schoolboy' and similar epithets unsuitable for a senior player.) Less predictable was young Keegan's answer to my question, "Which type of game do you like the best?" His knock-you-over-with-a-feather reply was "Five days; the other games are too short."

The boy's astonishing choice flew directly in the face of the received wisdom of the past ten years or so from clubs, pubs, online cricket forums, and wherever cricket is discussed. The views and prognostications nearly always sound the same: the twenty first century wants fast action, instant gratification, immediate thrills; Test cricket is going to disappear, the millennials just find it too boring; formats will keep growing shorter and shorter, see, we're down to a 'Hundred' already; cricket won't be too different from baseball in the end; and so on and so forth.

This is not the place to start debating 'Whither cricket?', '*Quo vadis* cricket?' or whatever learned phrase for the game's future direction you may prefer. The point is that I have subsequently heard a few other boys of around Keegan's age express the same format preference as him, though there are admittedly also many who go for the easier thrills and spills of T20.

We know about the characteristics of the so-called Millennials generation. But they have been succeeded by Generation or Gen Z, my young friend Keegan's 'age cohort'. The sociocultural researchers who are stewards of these terms will probably disagree, but for me, the Gen Z's are perceptibly different from the Millennials – more patient, more appreciative, more open to action taking time to unfold. I'd never have expected this development, but young Keegan's favourite cricket format was just one symptom of it that I've observed. Life is full of surprises; cricket is a slice of life, and likewise full of surprises. Support from Keegan's more receptive generation may just help give Test cricket a new lease of life, boosted possibly by England's 'revolution of 2022' (**Bite 27**). To adapt Mark Twain's reaction on reading his own obituary, reports of Test cricket's demise are much exaggerated.

# 51. THE GAME MUST GO ON

There'd been some kind of disturbance, and the players were actually given the option whether to continue the international match or not. They opted to go on. I wish I could remember the details, but they escape my memory. I thought for years it was after the first of the two riots at the Georgetown 5th ODI in 1998, (the second was at the very end when Steve Waugh set out on perhaps the most difficult run of all time, a match- and series-tying third as fans swarmed around him on the pitch and one tried to steal his bat). But the Georgetown facts don't fit; there was no question of not finishing the match. Sadly, only one part of the report of the game I have in mind has stayed with me (though I'm sure it was an international). A player interviewed afterwards, asked why they'd chosen to play on, replied, "Our hearts weren't in it; but we went on *for the sake of cricket.*"

Lower the average age of the players by some fifteen years and the status of the match by almost as large a gulf as cricket encompasses. This one I remember vividly. My nephew was playing for his school Under-10 team one Saturday. The game, scheduled to start at eight-thirty in the morning, was delayed by some unexpected factor and only got under way at twelve-thirty p.m. This had serious implications, because there was a heat wave in February, already the hottest month in the southern summer, and temperatures by noon were in the high 30s (or past 100 F.) and rising.

The two teacher-umpires had doubts about even letting their

mostly nine-year-old charges play in such heat, and as the afternoon grew hotter, they wanted to call off the game. Parents in deck-chairs watching the game agreed. But the boys themselves begged and pleaded to be allowed to carry on. One mother actually went onto the field to take her son off, but he implored her to let him stay. The boys were asked time and again if they wanted to stop, but they were adamant about playing the game through to its end. Nobody wanted to issue them an actual diktat.

The match, in my fancy, began to take on a kind of epic quality: not the contest between two very junior teams, but the struggle between cricket itself and the elements – in this case the scorching African heat. And in any epic struggle, the combatants need supply lines. One parent went off to fetch several packs of bottled water and energy drinks. Parents (and one uncle) shuttled the drinks out to the players far more often than the $12^{th}$ man would in a senior match, in fact almost at the end of every over. The same mother who'd wanted to take her son off, produced a tube of sun cream and squeezed some out for all the flushed young warriors. Some parents soaked handkerchiefs in water and took them out to the boys to knot around their heads -though they proudly insisted on keeping their school caps on over the improvised wet bandanas.

At last the match ended – played to a proper one-innings finish, with both sides all out within around four hours, as will happen in an Under-10 game. Even then, with the sun still merciless, the boys didn't scuttle into the shade immediately. First they solemnly formed two lines and clasped one another's small sunburnt hands, carrying out the courtesies as players do at every level.

My nephew, questioned about the stubborn persistence as no

doubt the other 21 boys also were, answered with the simple but deeply felt words of a nine-year-old. "We wanted to play. It was very hot, but we wanted to carry on. We wanted to finish the game. I'm glad we did. Thank you for helping us finish the game."

Do I even need to draw a conclusion from these two incidents, one only fuzzily remembered, the other very clearly? The international players who carried on "*for the sake of cricket*" were on the same page as those young boys whom I watched willingly suffering the furnace. Cricket is an abstract ideal for which its participants will endure much. With this level of commitment, the game must go on, in all senses. Each individual match will be played out as far as humanly and practically possible. The sport itself endures, world without end. I have no doubt at all that cricket will survive for as long as humans play sport.

## 52. TO CONCLUDE: THOUGHTS ON THREE CRICKET POEMS
## *(Actually just short bits of the poems that are still relevant)*

**i.** *"There's a breathless hush in the close tonight/Ten to make and the match to win/A bumping pitch and a blinding light/An hour to go and the last man in..."*

Never mind the rest of the poem by Sir Henry Newbolt. We all recognise the situation immediately. It is part of cricket more now than ever: the nail-biting finish, down to the wire, spectators on the edge of their seats, players just as tense as the fans and straining every fibre to swing the result their team's way. Of course it happens more often in white-ball cricket and especially T20, but this is due to the artificial constraints of limited overs. Somehow the most exciting tight finishes are in Test matches, when, uniquely in sport, a draw rather than a tie is an option and is often what one team is fighting grimly for. So these four lines are completely relevant to cricket today; you still occasionally hear them quoted when the finish justifies it.

**ii.** The other classic cricket poem I'm about to quote needs a bit of context to understand it. The poet, Francis Thompson, has lived in Lancashire for most of his life, but is now resident in London for whatever reason. He still thinks of Londoners as 'Southrons' – northern England dialect for southerners. One day he's invited to watch Middlesex hosting his beloved Lancashire at Lord's. But when he thinks of the prospect of seeing the familiar Lancashire emblem of the Red Rose on the field again, he finds he can only think of the Lancastrian players he watched in his youth, and decides not to go to the game.

*It is little I repair to the matches of the Southron folk/Though my own red roses there may blow/It is little I repair to the matches of the Southron folk/Though the red roses crest the caps I know/For the field is full of shades as I near the shadowy coast...*

Then it becomes too nostalgic and sentimental to go on; you get the drift. Becoming personal now, I have to emphasise that most aspects of Mr Thompson's dilemma do not apply to me and probably don't to you. Like him, I have moved from the north to the south-east of my country. But unlike him, I go to watch cricket with alacrity when there are familiar flowers on one side's caps: in my case, not roses but proteas (red in nature most often, but golden on the cricket emblem in line with SA's national sporting colours of green and gold). The coast that I near for this purpose is anything but shadowy; it's known as the Sunshine Coast (in the Eastern Cape province). The field is not full of shades for me, but is full of cricketers in action and very much alive. I do often picture former players in my mind's eye, but without Mr Thompson's nostalgia. It happens generally when a current player reminds me of a forerunner by something in his batting style, bowling action, mannerisms or whatever. This is part of my whole idea of cricket, as I said at the start: continuity amid change; a vibrant present but with the past as an ever-present backdrop.

    **iii.** *"Have you ever felt the urge to write/Of all the cricket that has blessed your sight?"*

This question-cum-challenge doesn't come from any famous poet, but was put in poetic form by a friend to Edmund Charles Blunden, a writer who could be described as a 'cricket philosopher'. The result was Blunden's *Cricket Country,* which I regard as the book that, more than any other, is appreciative and evocative of all the game's treasures and glories. Much of it is sheer poetry in prose. I would never begin to compare myself with Blunden; but these Bites have been an attempt to accept the same challenge that he did. I do hope you have enjoyed reading them as I enjoyed writing them. Viva Cricket, the real Beautiful Game.

*Cricket to us was more than play; it was a worship in the summer sun* – Edmund Blunden.

## -- STUMPS --